Woolwich. Guide to the Royal Arsenal. (Reprint of "Warlike Woolwich.") Tenth thousand.

William Thomas Vincent

Woolwich. Guide to the Royal Arsenal. (Reprint of "Warlike Woolwich.") Tenth thousand.
Vincent, William Thomas
British Library, Historical Print Editions
British Library
1885
168 p. ; 8°.
10350.bbb.42.

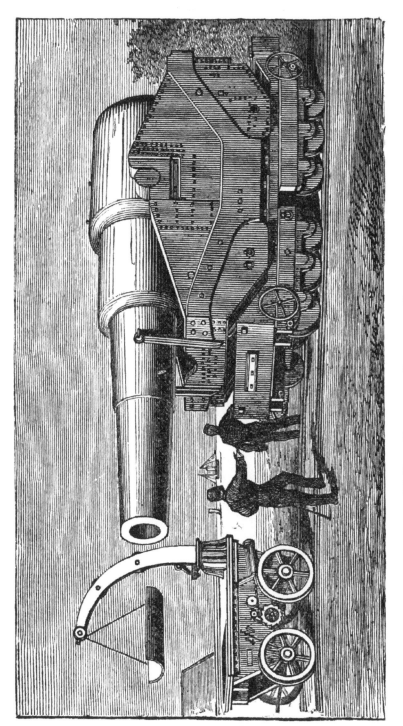

80-Ton Gun and Loading Derrick.

SYNOPSIS

OF THE

PRINCIPAL SIGHTS

AT

WOOLWICH ARSENAL.

ROYAL LABORATORY.

Main Factory :
  Bullet and Lead Squirt-
    ing Machines.
Model Room :
  Shells, Rockets, &c.
  Torpedoes.

Cartridge Factory :
  Percussion Caps.
  Rolling Brass, &c.
  Making Clay Plugs.
Shell Foundry.
Shell Factory.

ORDNANCE STORES.

War Trophies.
Shot Ground.

Harness Store.
T Pier.

ROYAL GUN FACTORIES.

Boring and Rifling.
Coiling.
Pattern Room.
Forges & Steam Hammers.

Rolling Mills.
The Great 40-ton Hammer.
Monster Guns.
Shrinking.

ROYAL CARRIAGE DEPARTMENT.

Wheel Factory :
  Copying Machines.
  Wheel Machinery.
  Endless Band Saw.
Field Carriage Shop.

Main Factory :
  Circular Plane.
Main Forge :
  Forging Machinery.
  3,000-ton Press.

Model Room.

WOOLWICH.

GUIDE

TO THE

ROYAL ARSENAL, &c.

By Wm. Thos. VINCENT.

TENTH THOUSAND.

CONTENTS:

1. THE ROYAL ARSENAL.
2. THE ROTUNDA, BARRACKS, &c.
3. A TRIP TO WOOLWICH.
4. HISTORY OF WOOLWICH.
5. HISTORY OF ROYAL ARSENAL.
6. HISTORY OF CHARLTON.
7. HISTORY OF PLUMSTEAD.
8. HISTORY OF SHOOTERS' HILL.
9. CROSSNESS OUTFALL.
10. GEOLOGY, &c.
11. TABLE OF DISTANCES.
12. PARLIAMENTARY ELECTIONS.
13. CHRONOLOGICAL TABLES.

WOOLWICH : A. W. AND J. P. JACKSON, PRINTERS AND PUBLISHERS, "KENTISH INDEPENDENT" OFFICE.

LONDON : SIMPKIN, MARSHALL, & CO., STATIONERS' HALL COURT, LUDGATE HILL.

THE want of a good Guide Book to Woolwich, a book not too erudite or elaborate—neither too complicated for rapid consultation, nor too heavy to carry—a book in fact which "he who runs may read" and appeal to for information as he would to a living guide at his elbow; this is the chief want which this little work is designed to supply. In the portion devoted to our great national workshop, the Royal Arsenal, and, in fact, wherever it assumes the character of Guide, I have studied first of all to make it simple, brief, and plain, so that the visitor may take in its information at a glance. To simplicity I have sometimes sacrificed even interesting, though often technical, details—some of which, however, will be supplied, where necessary, in smaller type, for perusal or rejection at will. But in its historical and descriptive chapters, which are written to be read at leisure, I have indulged my pen without feeling bound by any such restraint, and if at any time I fall into the opposite extreme of prolixity, I trust that the deep and almost affectionate interest I feel in my subject may plead my pardon. I am not, however, without hope that my book may contain much that is new and interesting, not only to those who have associations with Woolwich, permanent or casual, but to the general reader.

The Chronological Section, in which I have embraced in order of date all the remarkable events which have taken place in connection with Woolwich, from the most remote periods of history, will, I hope, be found of sufficient value to justify the labour I have expended in its production. It has necessitated a careful study of some thousands of newspapers and other records in various places, but I am under a special obligation to the officials of the British Museum for the courtesy and attention I have received at their hands; I am under deep obligations to Mr. Thomas Morgan, and other old inhabitants for the valuable and interesting information they have given me; I have also had the advantage of consulting files of *The Kentish Independent* since its publication at Woolwich in 1848, and I have presumed to lay under contribution some able antiquarian notes by J. Hewitt, Esq., the eminent archeologist, and Lieutenant Grover, Royal Engineers; besides being highly favoured in having, through the kindness of Mr. R. Rixon, original and precious records written by Mr. Wells, who, in his far-off home in New Zealand, has retained a fond remembrance of his native town. To the various officials connected with the Government establishments I take the opportunity of returning thanks for much kindness and help extending over a series of years, and to the gentlemen who constitute what are usually called the "local authorities"—in fact, to all my friends —my gratitude is due for the ready information I have received whenever and wherever it has been requested.

WILLIAM THOMAS VINCENT.

INTRODUCTION TO PRESENT EDITION.

A favourable reception and rapid sale have so far justified the production of this unpretentious work. In the present edition an attempt has been made to rectify some errors and remedy some defects; and the kind indulgence of the public must be relied upon to cover all remaining imperfections.

WILLIAM THOMAS VINCENT.

INDEX.

	Page
ABBEY WOOD..	78, 131
Academy, Rl. Mil., 53,68,92,103,109,144,145	
— In Arsenal	117
Accidents, Peace Fête	94
— Precautions against ..	48
— Remarkable	50
Almshouses	106
American Breechloaders	28
Ants, Indian	47
Armstrong Guns	29
Army Service Corps	55
Arsenal, Admission to	9
— Appendix	48
— Chapel	95, 117
— Fortification of ..	111
— Guide to	9
— History of.. ..	109
— Map of, Ancient	108
— Origin of Name ..	75, 119
— Synopsis of Sights ..	8
Artillery, Royal	56
— Origin of	90, 91
— Barracks .. 54, 56, 91, 92, 193
— Barracks in Arsenal 91, 112, 117
— Institution	56
BAND, Royal Artillery ..	59
Baptists, the	95
Barking..	76, 77
Barrack Field	59, 93
Beanfeast	53
Beating the Bounds	83
Beresford Square ..	97, 112
Bhurtpore Gun	58, 125
Bird's Nest, curious	47
Bloomfield, Lord	107
— Poet	134
Boring Mills	33
Borgard, General ..	112, 115
Boundaries	83, 135
Bowater, Mr. 85, 93, 100
— Pond, Accident ..	88
Boxer's Parachute	16, 17
Brass Foundry .. 11, 112, 116
Brook Hill	135
Bullet-making..	13
Bull Inn	133
Burrage Town	127
CADETS, distinguished ..	69
— Bathing	117
Cap Factory, percussion ..	19
Carpenters	18, 41
Catholics, Roman	95
Cambridge Barracks.. ..	69
Camp, The	69
Carriage Department .. 40, 112, 113
Cartridges	14, 19, 48
Cemetery, Woolwich.. ..	104, 146
— Charlton	123
— of Guns	28, 31
Charlton, History of.. ..	121
— Church ..	121, 122
— Road made ..	100
Charlotte Rees	86
Chemical Department ..	20
Chronological Tables ..	143
Churches and Chapels .. 59, 94, 122

	Page
Church Rates .. — ..	86, 147
Coaches to London	97
Coiling Mills	29
Colefields	85, 126
Commissioners, Board of ..	104, 144
Congreve, General	63
Congregationalists, The ..	95, 96
Control Department... ..	24
Convicts.. .. .. 51, 119, 147
Cooperage	19
Copying Machines	42
Coroner..	144
Cottages, Soldiers'	125
Cricket Ground	59
Crimean Memorial	57
Crossness 128, 136, 148
DE LUCY, Richard ..	78, 131
Departments, Arsenal ..	10
Depot Barracks	55
Dial Square	11, 116
Dick Turpin	133
Distances, Table of	166
Dockyard, Woolwich ..	72, 88
— Closing of .. 73, 90, 149
— Extension ..	98, 145
— Church	69
Dover Volunteers	29
Drainage, Woolwich	104
— The main	136
Duel prevented	104
ENGINEERS, Royal	54, 146
Enon Chapel	95
Epitaphs 87, 88, 130
Elections	164-5
Execution at Shooters' Hill ..	134
Experiment, ludicrous ..	50
Explosions .. 146, 146, 147, 147, 148, 148
FIELD GUNS	32
Fish Torpedo	17
Forest, submerged	77
Frazer Gun 29, 30, 35
Fuzes	15
GAS introduced	94
— Works, Arsenal	52
Garibaldi	148
Garrison, Woolwich	54
— Church	72, 81
Geology	141
Golgotha of Guns	28, 31
Granby, Marquis	103
Grand Depot	55
Gravel pits	124, 142
Great Harry	88
Green's End	97, 112
Greenviz (Greenwich) ..	76
Greenwich College	71
Grimaldi, Clown	88
Guns, Ancient.. .. 53, 58, 67
— Curious 50, 53, 63
Gun Factories..	28, 112
— Ground	52, 111
— Foundry, Brass .. 11, 110, 112, 116
HANGING WOOD .. 99, 100, 124
Harness Store	26
Harry Grace de Dieu	89
Holidays at Arsenal	53

	Page
Horn Fair	123
Hospital, Female	60
Hospitals, Military	55, 69, 92, 93
Hulviz (Woolwich)	75
INFANT, The Woolwich	31
— School	9, 34
Institution, Artillery	56
JOLLY Shipwrights	99
KIDBROOKE	123
LABORATORY, Royal	48, 110, 112
Leslie, Fredk., actor	166
Lessness Abbey	78
Little Heath	99, 100
Local Board	104, 146
London, Carriage to	74, 96
Lovelace, poet	88
Love Lane	98
MAGAZINES, powder	48
Mallet's Mortars	25
Maltese Gun	11
Map of Old Woolwich	101
— Royal Arsenal	108
Marine Barracks	69, 99, 146
Mary Rose, The	52
Marquis Granby	103
Maudslay, engineer	88, 148
Maxey	127
Messroom, R.A.	57
Military Train	55
Mineral Well	69
Moorfields Explosion	114
Mutiny of Artillery	92
Murders	87, 144, 145, 147, 147
NEWSPAPERS, Old	98, 100, 125, 133
North Woolwich	86
OMNIBUSSES, old	97
Ordnance Stores	24
PALLISER Shells	17, 21, 22, 64
Paper Factory	19
Parker, Murder of	87
Parliamentary Elections	164
Parliamentary	165
Passage boats	97
Percival, Spencer	123
Percy, Dr.	95
Physical conformation	135
Pippins at Plumstead	143
Plumstead Churches	80, 126, 128
— History of	126
— Road, ancient	112
Police Station	93, 145
Population	105, 123, 126, 165
Proof and Practice Butts	49, 112
Presbyterians, The	95, 96
RAILWAYS	18, 74, 97
Recreation Rooms	57
Red Barracks	69
Rees, Charlotte	87
Relics of Woolwich	75, 77, 102
Repository	59, 93, 100
Revel, Ancient	91
Riding School	56
River Wall	78
Roads, Old	99, 123, 125, 131
Rockets	15
Rolling Mills	20, 36
Roman Catholics, The	95
Roman Docks	80, 131
— Era, the	77
— Pottery	75, 77
Ropemakers	90
Rope Walk	96, 144
Rotunda	62
Royal Visits	38, 89, 94, 102, 117, 148
Ruins, Abbey Wood	79
Rupert, Prince	111
Rupert's Tower	16, 100, 109, 113, 117
— Walk	112, 117
Russian War	120
SALE Yard	49
Sawmills	18, 41
Scenery	128
Schalch, Andrew	88, 110, 113, 116
School Board Elections	165
Select Committee	11
Severndroog Castle	133, 134
Shell Foundry	20
Shooters' Hill	128, 132, 141
Shrewsbury House	133
Sims Reeves	96
Steamboats	71
Steamboat Company	97
Steam-hammer	31, 36
Street fight	100
St. John's Church	96
Strike of Shipwrights	102
TABLE of Distances	166
T-Pier	26, 120
Telegraph Factories	72
Thames, River	105
Theatre, R.A.	57
Tombstones, curious	87, 88, 130
Tom Cribb	72, 87, 148
Tom Griffiths	87
Torpedoes	17, 49
Town Hall	93
Trinity Church	96
Trip to Woolwich	70
Trophies of War	25, 58
Turneries	28, 35
UNION, Woolwich	105, 131, 149
VALLEYS, The Seven	135
Vestry, old books	82, 129
WARREN, The	91, 110, 118
War with France	94
Warspite, The	72
Watering time	98
Watling Street	77
Wellington's Statue	25
Wellington Street	97
Wesleyans, The	95
Wheel Factory	41
Woolwich, History	75
— Fifty years ago	96
— Hundred years ago	98
— Thousand years ago	75
— Cage and Stocks	85
— Common	85, 93, 99
— Church	72, 81, 85, 99
— Churchyard	86, 104
— Parsonage	86
— View of in 1790	84
Wordsworth, poet	107
Workhouses	106, 130, 131

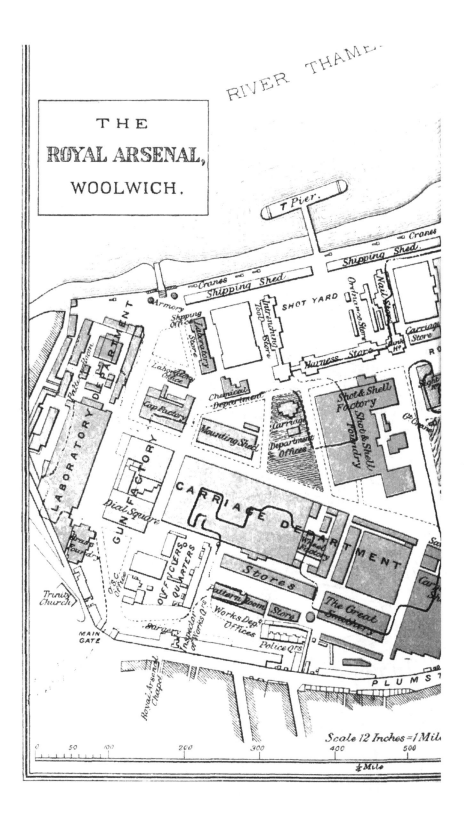

THE

ROYAL ARSENAL,

WOOLWICH.

RIVER THAMES

T Pier.

Scale 12 Inches = 1 Mile

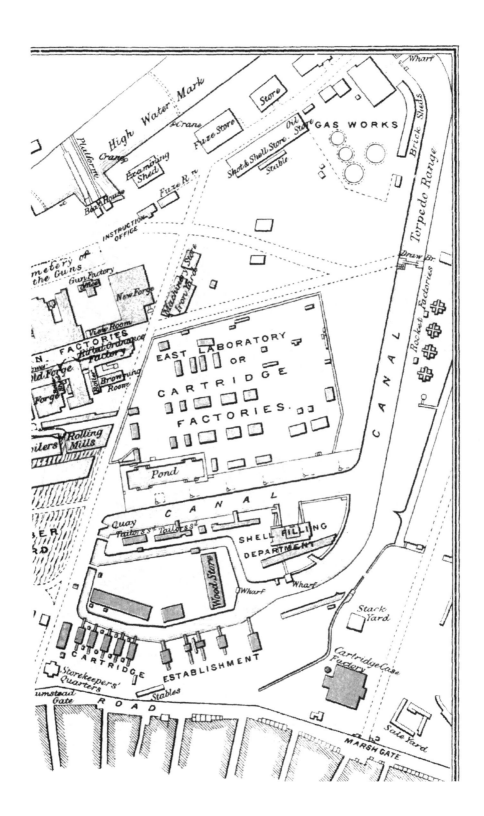

THE WOOLWICH INFANT SCHOOL, ROYAL ARSENAL.—May 20th, 1874.

GUIDE
TO THE
ROYAL ARSENAL.

——— : oo : ———

O gain admittance to the Royal Arsenal, visitors must be provided with a pass from the War Office. These passes can easily be obtained by personal application, or, in special cases, by letter, addressed to " The Secretary of State for War, Pall Mall, S. W.," stating who the persons are for whom the orders are required, and guaranteeing that they are British subjects. Foreigners must be provided with special permits, which, however, they will have no difficulty in obtaining through the representatives of their nation in London. Strangers unprovided with passes will always be refused admission by the police at the gates, but individuals acquainted with officers of the Establishment occasionally, by especial favour and good fortune, obtain cards

B

of admission on the spot. This, however, is generally by pre-arrangement, and it is always better to get the War Office authority direct. Those who come unprovided with this talisman will only waste time in attempting to succeed in entering the Arsenal without it. They had better make their way at once to the Common, and see the Museum at the Rotunda, which is described further on, and is well worth seeing; the pleasure of inspecting the Arsenal they must defer until some other time. Tuesday and Thursday in each week are visiting days, but occasionally special cards are given for other days.

In the Guide which follows, we have taken the route ordinarily pursued by visitors, as laid down in the accompanying plan, a route which, if taken under the direction of any one familiar with the place, occupies from two to three hours. Persons, however, who take an exceptional interest in the operations they may here witness, generally spend two or three hours before the interval for dinner (one till two o'clock) in going over part of the Arsenal, and return afterwards to complete the remainder at leisure. As some of the principal operations in the Royal Gun Factories are frequently timed to take place early in the afternoon, this arrangement is to be commended. It is advisable, if possible, to make early enquiry as to the time of day when interesting operations at the Gun Factories are expected, which is generally 3 p.m. One of each party has to sign his name in a book at the police office on the right of the Main Gate, and the visitors are then put in the direction of the Royal Laboratory to make the tour. They would then do wisely, unless accompanied by an expert conductor, to consult the following pages.

The Four chief divisions of the Royal Arsenal are—

The Royal Laboratory, which is principally devoted to the manufacture of *ammunition*, both for small arms and artillery, large and small;

The Royal Gun Factories, where the heavy guns are made;

The Royal Carriage Department, in which are produced gun carriages for land and naval service of all descriptions;

The Ordnance Store Department, in which are collected and warehoused warlike stores of all kinds, and issued as required for use.

Each of these departments is under the direction of a separate Superintendent, an officer selected from the Army on account of his special experience and other qualifications for the branch of the service to which he is appointed.

ENTRANCE GATES. Erected in 1829.

An inscription let into the interior wall of the west lobby, states that "This Entrance to the Royal Arsenal was planned, and this Gateway constructed, by order of General Viscount Beresford, G.C.B., G.C.H., Master General of the Ordnance, in the 10th year of the reign of His Majesty King George the Fourth, A.D. 1829." The entrance was formerly a little to the west, nearer the Guard room. By these gates and the next entrance in Plumstead Road, something like 10,000 workmen pass daily to and from their employment in the Arsenal. This is in time of peace ; but when, unhappily, the nation has been preparing for war, the number of workpeople has more than once reached nearly to 14,000. These war times are seasons of prosperity to Woolwich, but are invariably followed by periods of deep depression, owing to sudden reductions.

MALTESE GUN on the Green opposite the Gates.

This is a handsome brass culverin, brought from Malta, and is remarkable for its length, nearly 20 feet. It is of French manufacture, and dated 1607, bearing an inscription recording the names of the "grand conservators" who took part in its creation. It is mounted on a carriage made in the Royal Arsenal in 1827.

SELECT COMMITTEE OFFICES, &c.

In rear of this curious cannon are the Select Committee Offices connected with the department of the Director of Artillery and Stores. In these is transacted most of the business connected with the various experiments carried out by the scientific committees appointed by the War Office. The rest of the block of buildings consists of officers' quarters.

On the right may be seen the Surgery and Hospital, the School Room, where the Arsenal boys have to attend for stated hours, the Arsenal Mechanics' Institute, Police Barracks, &c.

On the left is the Engine House and Guard Room.

THE DIAL SQUARE (a branch of the Royal Gun Factories) occupies a position almost facing the entrance, and has a sun dial dated 1764 over the gateway.

It consists of various fitters and founders' shops, but is seldom visited by the public, except when there is some great casting to be made in the workshop at the back. This and the adjacent Brass Foundry were formerly the main buildings of the Royal Gun Factories, an establishment which has now gone further a-field to grow, as we shall presently see.

THE BRASS FOUNDRY, adjoining the Guard-room, is one of the oldest buildings at the Arsenal, but bronze guns are

no longer made, and the Foundry is chiefly devoted to the small castings required by the Laboratory Department.

The Foundry has a strange history, which will be found elsewhere in this book. Both inside and out it has a remarkable resemblance to a church, and there is an ancient furnace at the further end which may be seen as a curiosity. Note the quaint gun-shaped chimneys.

THE ROYAL LABORATORY DEPARTMENT.

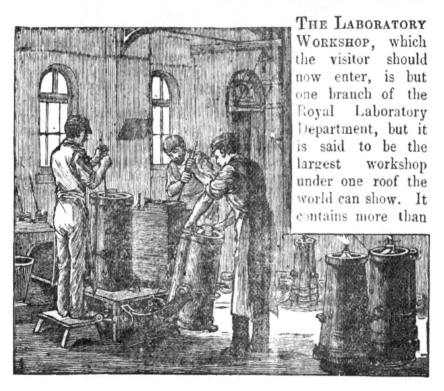

THE LABORATORY WORKSHOP, which the visitor should now enter, is but one branch of the Royal Laboratory Department, but it is said to be the largest workshop under one roof the world can show. It contains more than

SHOT AND SHELL CASTING.—Page 21.

---

five hundred lathes for the performance of various kinds of work, and some of the most perfect and extraordinary machinery ever produced. Overhead are 4,077 feet of revolving shafts, crossing and re-crossing, to give motion to the lathes, and a bewildering complication of endless bands fly about in all directions, to connect the shafts with the machinery. The motive-power for all this work is derived from two fine pairs of engines, in the south-east and south-west corners of the building.

BULLET MACHINE.

BULLET MAKING is the most interesting operation which engages the attention in this vast workshop.   Coils of solid lead rod, looking like ordinary lead pipe, are conveyed to machines of simple but ingenious construction, which bite off a piece the required length, and punch it into the shape of a hollow conoidal bullet, some being hollowed out at the head also, in order to give them greater length without increasing their weight. Boys at adjacent machines finish and perfect the bullets by inserting a clay plug in the base, and by other interesting processes rapidly performed.

The clay plug is to assist in expanding the bullet to make it fit the rifling of the barrel on discharge, and so avoid windage. At first iron plugs were used, but they sometimes were blown right through the bullet, and were replaced by boxwood, but clay of a peculiar kind is now substituted, and has several advantages besides cheapness.

The original bullet-machines, introduced by Sir J. Anderson, LL.D., though thought marvellous in their time, were complicated and cumbersome compared with these, which were invented and introduced by Mr. Davidson, manager of the department, about 1871.   The bullets, when made, are taken down to the East Laboratory, in the remotest part of the Arsenal, where visitors are excluded, and they are there made up into cartridges.   These cartridges are, generally speaking, of two kinds only, both for breech-loading rifles, viz., the Martini-Henry (small-bore) and the Snider (converted Enfield).   As both are constructed on the same principle, though slightly different in shape, it will be sufficient to describe the original, the Snider, quoting from a work on ammunition by Major Majendie, R.A., formerly Assistant Superintendent of the Department.

" The Boxer service cartridge for the Snider rifle consists of a case of thin brass, rolled into a cylinder, and covered with paper, by which the coil is cemented together.   The coiled case is fitted into a double base-cup of brass, with an iron disk forming the end of the cartridge which abuts against the breech-block of the rifle. The case is secured in its position by means of a rolled paper wad inside, which is squeezed out with great force against the sides of the case. The iron base is attached to the cartridge by means of the copper "cap-chamber," which contains the detonating arrangement; the cap-chamber, being riveted over at each end, holds the base tightly to the cartridge. The ignition is effected by means of a percussion cap, resting on a small shouldered brass anvil in the base of the cartridge. To explode the cap, it is necessary that the crown of the cap should be indented (by the striker of the rifle, for example), when the detonating composition is brought into contact with the anvil, and the flash passes through the fire hole at the bottom of the cap-chamber to the powder in the case. The top of the cartridge is closed by means of a small quantity of wool, over which is fitted the bullet. This bullet has four grooves or *cannelures* round it, which serve to carry the wax lubrication."

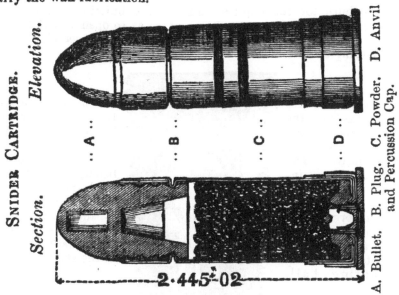

The cartridge for the Martini-Henry differs from this only in being bottle-shaped so as to contain the full charge of powder without elongating the cartridge or enlarging the bore of the rifle.

On an average a million cartridges per week are made in the Laboratory, but the producing power of the department is equal to three times that rate.

Lead-Squirting Room.—Through a doorway on the opposite side of the factory, the visitor may witness the process of "lead-squirting" as it is called, being the manufacture of the lead rod from which the bullets are made. Powerful hydraulic presses force the soft metal through a hole in the top, from which it may be seen to flow in an endless thread. The lead is melted in adjacent furnaces before being put into the press. Casting spherical bullets for case shot and various kinds of shell is also carried on in the "lead-squirting" shop.

Smith's Shops.

If the visitor has leisure, he may go through the "squirting room" to these places, and see the manufacture by steam hammers of the conical steel cups which form the heads of Shrapnel shell, besides other interesting operations.

Fuzes.—The fuzes made in the department are of several kinds, both of wood and metal. They are fixed in shells, in order to burst them when they reach the enemy's position, and may be divided into two classes—time fuzes and percussion fuzes.

Time Fuzes contain a slow burning composition, and may be "set" to burn for the requisite time before bursting the shell, by piercing their sides at a particular point, so as to open a vent for the burning composition when it has burned so many seconds, and instantly firing the shell.

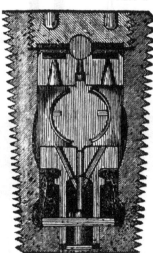

Percussion Fuzes are to explode the shell on its striking an object, whether far or near. The Pettman fuze, invented some years ago by Mr J. Pettman, a foreman in this department, may serve as a sample. It contains a small detonating ball, which is liberated from a safety cup by the shock of discharge, and when the shell comes into collision, the little ball is dashed violently against the interior of the fuze and explodes, thus igniting the bursting charge in the shell.

SECTION OF PETTMAN'S FUSE.

Rockets.—Returning to the "big shop," we may see something of the manufacture of rockets (rockets for saving life, and rockets for destroying it.)

The peculiarity of Hale's rocket (which has almost superseded the Congreve rocket) is that it is fired without a stick, the escape of the gas which gives it propulsion being also utilized to give it direction. The base contains three vents, prolonged in the shape of three curved shields. The pressure of the escaping gas against these shields causes the rocket to rotate, and by this means it is kept point foremost. These rockets were of great service in the forest battles of the Ashantee War.

The Life-saving Rocket (Boxer's) is fired with a stick, and has rope attached to it, which is used to throw over a ship in distress.

POWDER CASES.—As we walk down the west avenue, we see the presses at work corrugating the brass sheets of which powder-cases are made ; and in a small shop on our left, the rest of the operations connected with the manufacture and testing of these cases are performed, the tops and lids having previously been cast in the brass foundry. As a measure of precaution, brass or gun metal is always employed in lieu of iron wherever gunpowder is likely to be brought in contact, and various expedients are adopted for imparting strength to the softer metals, By corrugating the brass sides of these cases, their strength is six times multiplied.

GAUGERS.—The workmen busy in an enclosure at the northern end of the shop are employed to gauge-measure every article made in the department, as it is of the utmost importance that everything shall be true to size, sometimes to the two-thousandth part of an inch.

LABORATORY PATTERN ROOM.—We now pass out of the large workshop, and, crossing a yard, enter the Pattern Room Museum, where also are the printing and other offices. The original of this building was, according to tradition, Prince Rupert's palace, about the time of the Great Fire of London (1666), and it bears evidences of having been a palatial residence, though it has been at least once restored, and was formerly the Royal Military Academy.* In the entrance-hall are specimens of heavy shot and shell, rockets, &c., artistically arranged.

On the right is the principal model-room, which was once, probably, the saloon chamber. It is lofty, and is 60 feet in length. It is not necessary to explain the many objects of interest here exhibited, for lucid descriptions are appended to each model and specimen.

Take notice of Boxer's parachute light-ball † which, fired in the air, opens like an umbrella, suspending a vivid light, by which the enemy's position and his secret operations may be revealed, even in the dead of night.

---

* See "History of Royal Arsenal." † See Illustration.

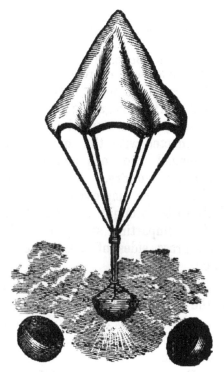

BOXER'S PARACHUTE LIGHT BALL.

Note also the sections of the cartridges, fuzes, and shells, a careful study of which, or even a glance, will explain their character better than any description. Examine the hard-headed Palliser shell, broken asunder to show the gradual alteration in the character of the metal by the chilling process, the point being hardened like steel by rapid cooling, and the rest cooled gradually to preserve its toughness.

In the room on the left, said to have been the dining hall, are exhibited a number of torpedoes. They are made to contain from 100 to 1,000 lbs. or more of gun-cotton, and, being fired either by contact or by electric communication with the shore, would inevitably prove the destruction of any ship which should venture near.

The *Whitehead "Fish Torpedo"* is also here exhibited. This mysterious engine of war is worked by compressed air, and will travel in a straight line for nearly a mile. Notwithstanding the continual loss of buoyancy caused by the consumption of air, it preserves, by an automatic arrangement, the required depth in the water, and can be set to rise or sink at any given number of yards in its range. The head is charged with gun-cotton, the air chamber occupies the tail end, and the little "Brotherhood" engines by which it is worked may be seen in the middle. The secret of the invention cost the English Government many thousands of pounds, and it is also possessed by Austria, Germany, Turkey, and Italy. The French and Russians have not acquired it, and America has contented herself with an imitation of an inferior description.

Harvey's Torpedo is another of the aggressive kind. It is attached by ropes at a certain angle to the ship's side, and the motion of the vessel through the water causes it to swerve off and strike an enemy at a considerable distance.

Models of cartridges for heavy guns, some of them resembling huge bolsters, but stuffed with coal dust or some other harmless material, are exhibited in cases against the walls; also smoke balls, ground-lights, &c. But we must hasten on, without even glancing at the dungeon-like vaults below (with walls 7 ft. thick), now used as old stores.

The Miniature Railway cannot fail to be remarked by the visitor on leaving the museum. Its gauge is but 18 in., the advantages of which are not only saving of cost and space, for it enables the little engines which run upon it to turn sharp angles and penetrate into the remotest corners of the establishment. The powder magazines far away in the Marshes, and all parts of the Arsenal are connected by this railway, on which passenger cars as well as goods trucks, some ingeniously constructed, so as to carry the most awkward objects, can travel. The plates of which it is mainly composed were cast in the Shell Foundry.

The Carpenter's Shop adjoins the Museum on one side, and the Tinman's Shop on the other. It is not usual, unless there is time to spare, to visit these; but mechanics will take an interest in a truly wonderful dovetailing machine in the carpenter's shop—a splendid specimen of ingenuity. A short inspection may also be made of

The Sawmills, on the opposite side of the yard, passing a series of corrugated iron sheds, used as workshops and timekeepers' offices. (In one of these is made the Whitehead "fish" torpedo.) In the Sawmills the visitor will see, and doubtless comprehend, the wonderful works of the circular saws, as well as the horizontal saws which are cutting immense trees into planks.

THE COOPER'S SHOP is above the Sawmills, and contains machinery for the manufacture of powder barrels, pails, and tubs of various kinds, at the rate of three or four thousands weekly.

THE CAP FACTORY.—Passing out of the Laboratory gate, we cross the road and enter the Cap Factory, formerly called the " Paper Factory," having been originally used for the manufacture of paper cartridge-cases. It is here that the interesting operations connected with the production of percussion caps are carried out, and some other work of a kindred character. The visitors will see long bands of sheet copper passed through a machine, which punches out circular-shaped pieces to make the caps, delivers them, fairly made, into a box below, and expels the copper band, perforated like a piece of lacework, on the opposite side.

Although gun caps and gun nipples were discarded together on the adoption of breech-loading rifles, large quantities of percussion caps have still to be made, because one is required to be placed inside every cartridge, together with the little anvil on which it is struck.* These anvils are made in the same way as the caps, by an adjacent machine, and the brass and paper discs which are employed in the base of the cartridge, are produced by a similar method. Each of these little machines will turn out about 30,000 per hour, or four millions per week !

A number of boys are employed in this factory, both down stairs and up stairs, finishing off the caps, and every one has to be examined to see that it is perfect. They are then taken away to the cartridge sheds in the East Laboratory, to be charged with the detonating composition.

CLAY PLUG MAKING.—A very peculiar and ingenious machine near the east end of the Cap Factory must not be overlooked. It is that by which clay, substituted for box wood, is shaped into the plugs used in the base of the bullets.

Upon a revolving plate are six corresponding groups of moulds, five of which are constantly at work, while the attendant cleans the sixth. Into one group of moulds powdered clay is dropped from a hopper above, and, thus loaded, it passes on to be succeeded by group No. 2. A series of rams descend and press the clay into solid plugs, which in the third stage are disgorged and swept off the table, while

---

* See Illustration, Page 15.

the moulds go on to be wiped down, and passed under a set of lubri-cators, to be greased ready for another supply of clay. The clay dust, which is of the common kind, and apparently devoid of moisture, is pressed immediately into plugs as hard as stone.

ROLLING MILLS.—Towards the back part of the shop are mills for rolling out the brass bands from which cartridge-cases are made. The brass is reduced from ingots about an inch in thickness to sheets which go 250 to the inch.

ANNEALING FURNACES, in which the brass bands are annealed, are behind this factory.

UPSTAIRS, if the visitor would see more of such work, he may witness the process of making the copper percussion tubes by which artillerymen fire their guns with a lanyard, and he will here notice the careful nicety with which all the most minute work is examined, lest by any possibility a defect might creep in, and by creating a miss-fire at a critical moment, lead, perhaps, to disastrous consequences.

CHEMICAL DEPARTMENT.—Emerging from the east door of the Cap Factory, we see before us on our left hand a neat and cheerful looking edifice, in which the chemists of the War Department prepare their deadly compounds. In this build-ing, which no one must enter without special authority, have been made some of the most remarkable discoveries in the science of chemistry, especially in its modern application to the art of war. The development of one agent alone—gun-cotton, within a few years, has been such as to bring lasting fame to this mar-vellous laboratory, but it is a subject beyond the province of a guide-book. Here also are tested various articles supplied to the Government by contract; and an extensive photographic depart-ment is attached, whose operators are constantly employed copy-ing by the sun's rays, guns and carriages, targets and machinery, and all the implements and appliances used in the Royal Arsenal. Photographs of every new pattern produced in any department have to be sent for inspection to the War Office, in London, and they are frequently sent to foreign stations for the instruction of the officials and workmen there employed.

Passing the front of the Carriage Department Offices on our right, and, not heeding for the moment the Ordnance Store Department on our left, we turn to the right hand for the

SHOT AND SHELL FOUNDRY.—The entrance to this building lies through a pair of noble gates of cast-iron, having screens of the same material and pattern to the office windows on either side. These gates and screens are probably the most beautiful specimens of their kind to be seen in England. On entering, the visitor will be somewhat startled by the grim contrast within; for, save the lurid glare of the molten metal streaming in cataracts from the furnaces, or, in seething cauldrons, borne through the gloomy shades of this Inferno, scattering their dross in brilliant fiery stars over the iron floor, all is black as night. But it is questionable whether there is another large foundry in existence so neat and so perfect,—ay, so cheerful, as this. The system of order, reduced almost to a science in this place, has made operations, naturally dirty, capable of being performed not only with comparative cleanliness and comfort to the workmen, but with immensely greater facility and ease. All the hard work is done by machinery, steam and hydraulic power being alike made subservient to man's will, and the little three-wheeled trucks which one may see running about doing all kinds of work, may be remarked for the vast improvement they have effected on the rough and primitive appliances seen in most foundries. The moulders and others here employed commence work at 6 a m., and continue without intermission until 4 p.m., when they have done for the day. The ordinary interval for meals are ignored, in order that the furnaces, once heated, may be kept at work without interruption.

The work performed in the Shell Foundry is the making of shot and shell. These are now a-days nearly all for rifled ordnance, and will consequently be seen to be conical in shape. The principal types are known as the " common " and the " Palliser." A common *shot* may be described as a solid iron cone (strictly speaking, it is cylindro-conoidal), but it is seldom used now except for practice. Common *shell* is of the same form, but made hollow to contain a bursting charge of powder, fired either with a percussion or time fuze.

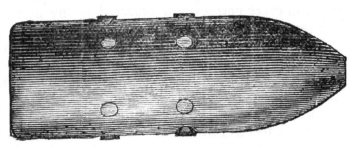

RIFLED COMMON SHELL.

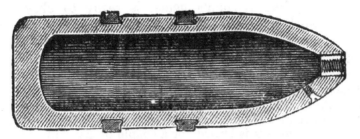

SECTION OF COMMON SHELL.

The 12 in. shells (*i e.* 12 in. in diameter) which may be seen in great
numbers, contain no less than 35 lbs. of powder. Against iron-clad
ships, however, these shells have little value, being made of "common" iron, and having little powder of penetration ; but against a
wooden ship, or one thinly plated, they may be most destructive. It
is said that the surrender of the *Alabama* to the *Kearsage*, in the
American war, has been attributed to one well delivered shell, which,
bursting like a mine in the body of the ship, spread death and destruction around. An eye witness on board the wooden ship *Congress*,
when attacked by the iron-clad *Merrimac*, in the same war, which
afforded the first practical test of modern naval warfare, thus describes the scene :

"The first shell that burst within the *Congress* killed every man at
the nearest gun ; another and another burst among the crew, and
the ship was soon a slaughter-house. Operations were now out of
question. The wounded were in crowds, horribly cut up. The ship,
too, was on fire ; the shells had kindled her woodwork in various
places. Nearly all the guns were dismounted, the bulkheads blown
to pieces, handspikes and rammers shivered, and the powder-boys all
killed. Everything was in fragments, black or red, burnt or bloody.
This horrible scene lasted about an hour and a half, and then she
struck."

The Palliser projectile is somewhat similar, though materially
dissimilar, in shape, and it is of a different character altogether. It
was invented by Major Palliser to pierce iron plates, and improved
by Mr. Davidson, it has been brought so near perfection as to leave
little to be desired. The most suitable iron having been found, the
shell is cast with its point in an iron chill, and its body in sand. The
metal at the point being by this means rapidly converted from the
fluid to the solid condition, becomes intensely hard, while the body,
cooling more slowly, retains the original toughness of the iron, and
keeps the shell from breaking up into fragments on striking. Palliser *shot* is so exceedingly hard and brittle, that after piercing an iron-
sided vessel it will break up into fragments like a shower of grape or
case shot. The Palliser *shell*, be it observed, may be fired without a
fuze, the heat engendered by concussion being alone sufficient to fire
the charge in the powder chamber.

CASTING PALLISER SHELL.—Men will be seen with
the moulds before them in a circle, in the centre of which is a

crane, which, like Alladin's genie, is ready to obey, and is always at work helping one or other of the group around him. The mould is prepared close by in a most ingenious manner, the stud holes being printed in by a mechanical arrangement which allows the pattern to be drawn out after the mould is made.

The sand mould, being complete, is fixed on an iron chill, and the casting taken. It is " fed" with more metal for some time, and when sufficiently firm, it is taken to the " cooling ground." on the right of the entrance, where it is buried for a couple of days in order that it may not cool too rapidly and crack.

ENORMOUS GRINDSTONES, driven by steam power, are employed to grind down the Palliser projectiles to gauge, for the metal is too hard to be turned in a lathe. These grindstones are unique of their kind. This work, like most of the other operations in this department, must be rather unpleasant.

THE FURNACES are a sight to see, and the tall CHIMNEY SHAFT at the back, which supplies the furnaces with draught, may be noticed as the highest in the Arsenal. It is taller than the monument of London, being 220 feet in height, and the stone coping at the top is said to weigh 17 tons.

SHRAPNEL SHELL, which should have been seen in the Pattern Room, may be here mentioned and briefly described.

The Shrapnel shell has a wooden head enclosed in a steel cup. The body is of cast iron, weakened internally by grooves, and it is filled with a number of bullets. The powder chamber is in the rear, so that when the fuze fires it, the bullets are driven forward with considerable impetus, and the shell bursts into fragments. Artillerists describe the effect of this shell as carrying forward the muzzle of the gun to within pistol shot of the enemy. By no other means can a shower of bullets be discharged into the ranks of the foe at such a long range.

Of *Segment Shell* and *Spherical Projectiles* (the old " cannon ball," with which England used to fight her battles) we need not speak ; a few may be seen about, but they are practically obsolete.

THE SHELL TURNERY adjoins the Shell Factory, being, in fact, under the same roof. The first thing which should strike the eye on entering is the *testing* of Palliser shell by water, and of common shell by steam—remarkable processes. The workmen are busy in all directions, and with machines of all descriptions, driving the bronze studs into the dovetailed hollows of the shells, turning, drilling, and " bushing ;" rifling the studs to give them the proper set in the rifle-grooves of the gun, and manifold other operations which speak for themselves.

Since the system was introduced of rotating shot and shell by means of gas checks (discs of copper attached to the base of the projectile) the use of studs has been gradually discontinued.

The official "Treatise on Ammunition" may be consulted for further details connected with the manufactures of this Department.

Passing through this shop into the open air once more, we cross to the stone archway of the

ORDNANCE STORE DEPARTMENT.

THE SHOT GROUND.

THE extensive and striking range of buildings which extend the whole length of the western wharf are the Ordnance Stores, which are continued in less pretentious edifices along the east wharf also; besides having extensive branches in the Dockyard, connected now by a line of railway, *via* the North Kent, and in communication also by steam-craft on the river. Everything required by the Army, in peace or war, can be supplied at a moment's notice from these wonderful storehouses, which are constantly being refilled from the Manufacturing Departments, or by orders upon private contractors. Guns and gun carriages; shot, shell, and cartridges; waggons, carts, and harness; barrack and stable furniture; tents and tables; brooms, brushes, pails, and all the paraphernalia of a soldier's equipment—all pass in and out of the "control" of this department, under systematic regulations. The department is a branch of the army, and connected with it is the Army Service Corps and other non-combatant regiments.

TROPHIES OF WAR.—Before entering the archway, we notice on either side several foreign guns captured in war. Most conspicuous are two Russian bronze cannon, mounted on the carriages they occupied when taken at Sebastopol during the Crimean War of 1854-6. The muzzles and sides of these guns show many a sore where they were struck by the shot and shell of the western invaders during that memorable and bravely-borne siege. Some round shot, which likewise bear evidences of active service, are also of Russian origin, having been some of those fired at our troops from the Redan, Malakoff, and Garden Batteries. Two iron guns from the Crimea stand at the back of this archway, and a number of Russian 13-in. shell lie about. The bronze guns and mortars arranged in the corners are specimens of old fashioned English ordnance. The bronze guns resting on sleepers before the entrance are Chinese, having been captured at the Taku Forts during the last war. Two of them bear the names of their captors, together with grandiloquent sentences inscribed upon them in Chinese. Each of these guns weighs about five tons, and is worth, merely as old metal, about £400. They are exquisitely made, and display, as the Chinese are apt to do, an intelligent notion of art, a hundred years after date.

Through the archway, and beyond another arch to the left, may be seen (with an ugly wound in its back) a specimen of Chinese brass ordnance with an iron lining, betraying a dim conception of the steel tube with which England now protects the throats of her " Infants."

DUKE OF WELLINGTON'S STATUE.—Before us, as we enter the realms of the Ordnance Store Department, we see a stone statue of His Grace the Duke of Wellington, of glorious memory. This was brought from the Tower of London, and placed here about 1860. It is of life size, and the features are a faithful likeness of the " Iron Duke." The guns and shot lying on either side of it are Chinese, and were brought from Hong Kong in 1866.

MALLET'S MORTARS.—The visitor has, no doubt, observed at several points on the route enormous spherical iron shells. These were made in 1857, by authority of Lord Palmerston, at the suggestion of Mr. Mallet, C.E., who proposed to fire them from a gigantic mortar, one of which may be seen standing as a trophy opposite the T Pier, close by the spot we have arrived at.

There were two of these mortars made, of iron staves and hoops, something like a barrel, and the writer saw a number of the shells fired from one of them at the range in the Marshes, in the year they were produced. The shells, which are 3 ft. in diameter, and weigh more than a ton each, were fired high into the air, and fell with such velocity, that some of them were buried 35 feet in the earth, where they still remain, the expense of digging them out being more than their value. It has been suggested that they will serve to astonish some geologist of the future, but as an experiment they were a failure. The mortar cracked ; but if it had been otherwise, its utility would have been doubtful. The increase of shell power, to an extent almost unlimited, has been found in another direction. The mortar which stands in the shot ground, was christened " Big Will," as a *compliment* to Lord Palmerston. One of the shells arranged in a trophy before it, informs us that it was fired at Woolwich on the 19th of October, 1857, that the distance it travelled was 2,644 yards (a mile and a half), with a charge of 70 lbs. of powder, penetrating the ground where it fell more than 10 yards. The weight of the shell is 2,548 lbs., to which should be added a bursting charge of 480 lbs., and the mortar weighs no less than 41 tons.

THE SHOT GROUND.--Here are arranged pyramids of shot and shell, of all kinds, shapes, and sizes, forming a grand spectacle which need not be described. (See Illustration, page 24.)

THE WHARF.—We may now glance up and down the wharf, which extends along the whole river front of the Arsenal, a length of more than a mile.

Here are often to be seen ships loading with the material of war, or stores, for the various garrisons at home and abroad ; and others unlading articles worn out or obsolete, which have been brought home to the great emporium—some to be sold at the monthly sales of old stores, some to be repaired, and others to be melted down into new shapes. At the T pier, as it is called from its shape, troops embark and disembark, and Royalty itself has often used it for the same purpose, on which occasions the hoops stretched over it support a handsome awning, its asphalte floor is thickly carpeted, and it is converted into a beautiful corridor. Her Majesty Queen Victoria and all her Royal Family have several times landed and embarked at this pier, the rest of the journey between here and London being performed by road, or by means of the North Kent Railway, a branch of which brings the Royal train to the very foot of the pier. The Emperor of Russia availed himself of the Royal Arsenal Railway when he visited Woolwich on the 20th of May, 1874, one of the greatest days in the annals of the town, greater even than that dazzled by the resplendent vision of the Shah of Persia the year before.

In dark contrast may be named the 11th of July, 1879, when the remains of the ill-fated young soldier, who was once Prince Imperial of France, were landed at the T Pier, re-coffined in the octagonal armoury near the west causeway, and conveyed by military escort to the home of the widowed Empress at Chiselhurst.

The *New Iron Pier*, for the shipment of heavy guns, runs out opposite the Royal Gun Factories, and is a fine work of its kind. The hydraulic crane upon it has a lifting power of over 100 tons.

HARNESS STORES.—It cannot be expected that the visitor will pass through all the great storehouses on the three floors of the Ordnance Store Department. One will suffice as a specimen of the whole, and that usually selected is the Harness Store. This is reached by a flight of stairs from the corner of the shot ground, near the departmental offices.   Here are always ready sets of harness for ten thousand horses—saddles and bridles, collars and traces, all neatly and even ornamentally arranged; while bits and curbs hang from the ceiling in countless festoons, and columns of stirrups are stacked up on either side.

Some curious specimens of harness are to be seen near the first front window.

1. An Abyssinian saddle and trappings, all of raw hide, said to have belonged to King Theodore.

2. An Ashantee saddle, covered with goatskin untanned, brought home with the spoils from Coomassie.

3. A camel's pack saddle from Damascus.

The visitor will walk through the whole length of these storehouses, passing over a bridge, from which a good general view of the shot ground and wharf is obtained. After turning to the left over another bridge, and passing through the Cavalry Harness Store, he should now descend by a door on the left hand to *terra firma* once more.

He will pass by other stores and buildings, including

THE HYDRAULIC ENGINE HOUSE, from whence power is supplied to all the cranes and machinery on the wharf and piers;

THE CHAIN CABLE TESTING HOUSES, where ropes and chains are tried; and

THE WEIGH BRIDGE OFFICE, at which loaded carts and waggons are accurately weighed.

The visitor will then pass at once to

THE ROYAL GUN FACTORIES.

THE CEMETERY.—Before reaching the world-famous establishment which bears the name of the Royal Gun Factories, we pass by a row of elm trees, under which we see a remarkable

LATHE IN TURNERY.—Page 35.

park of dead artillery, which has been called "The Cemetery." Here are collected together the fragments of cannon of all kinds, which have burst either at proof or on service—guns, for the most part, which have been submitted for trial by private inventors, and broken down under the test; but some of them, guns good and true, doomed from their birth to be sacrificed in the cause of science, and "tested to destruction." Here lie the black and shattered corpses of good and bad together, with mostly a brief epitaph, recording (more truthfully than epitaphs are wont to do) their history, and the manner of their death, with the number of rounds they endured before they perished

Six enormous bottle-shaped guns, which lie nearest the river, have a characteristic story to tell of commercial shrewdness. During the Crimean War, when breech-loading cannon was just being talked about, an American came over and submitted to the War Office a system of breech-loading which seemed to be the very thing wanting. He was ordered to make half-a-dozen guns at once, and his proposal to supply them by weight, at a mere trifle per pound, was regarded as a liberal arrangement. But when the guns were sent home, the Minister of War found that he had been outwitted. The manufacturer had heaped the iron in tons upon his guns, which from their enormous bulk were utterly useless ; but the maker had served his own purpose, and the sum which he had to be paid, when the "article" came to be weighed, was about ten times its value. However, he was paid, and nothing said about it, but the duped minister (he is now dead) could never bear the name of breech-loading guns afterwards. They have never been fired, and probably never will be

The fragments of the 32-pdr. which burst and killed two unfortunate volunteers at Dover in 1860 also lie in this Golgotha of the Guns.

THE COILING MILLS.—We commence our inspection of the Royal Gun Factories at the Coiling Mills in the East Forge. Furnaces 200 feet in length, stretch away down the whole length of the forge, and sometimes project, by a temporary arrangement, out through the further wall and across the rear road. Iron bars, of which the coils are to be made, lie on rollers before the door, ready to be run into the furnace. In this they are heated almost to a white heat, the temperature of the bar being regulated to an extreme nicety, so as to ensure the maximum of flexibility with the minimum of elasticity. At the mouth of the furnace is a revolving core or mandril, upon which there is a catch, which seizes one end of the bar, draws it out like a "snake of fire from a den of flame," and winds it round and round in a glowing spiral. This is one of the coils from which " Woolwich" guns are built up on the system invented by Mr. R. S. Fraser, Deputy Assistant Superintendent of the department. The best time to visit the coiling mills (or the Gun Factories altogether) with the hope of seeing a grand sight, is between two and three in the afternoon ; but for certain information on this point, the visitor had better make enquiries at the time.

In a lecture at the Royal Artillery Institution, Major Stoney, late Assistant Superintendent of the Royal Gun Factories, describes the principles of the coiling system, first introduced by Sir William Armstrong, as follows :—

" First, in arranging the fibre of the iron in the several parts so as best to resist the strain to which they are respectively exposed ; thus the walls or sides of the guns are composed of coils with the fibre running round the gun, so as to enable the gun to bear the transverse strain of the discharge without bursting, whilst the breech end is fortified against the longitudinal strain, or tendency to blow the breech out, by a solid forged breech-piece with the fibre running along the gun. Secondly, in shrinking on the successive parts together with tensions so regulated that each part shall do its due proportion of work on the discharge of the piece ; thus the outer coils contribute their fair share to the strength of the gun, whereas in an ordinary homogeneous gun the inner portions receive the brunt of the explosion, whilst the exterior ones are hardly affected by it at all.

" By a combination of these two principles, a gun is obtained which may be calculated to be twice as strong as a gun of the same weight and shape made out of a solid forging.

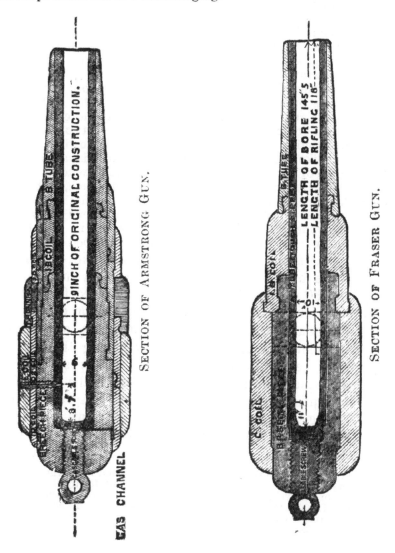

SECTION OF ARMSTRONG GUN.

SECTION OF FRASER GUN.

"The 'Woolwich' guns built on this system, and lined with toughened steel, are sound and strong; but from the fine iron used, and the great number of exquisitely finished coils, and a forged breech-piece, their manufacture was very costly; and, as it was probable that several heavy guns would be required, the War Office pointed out the desirability of adopting some cheaper plan. Accordingly, the attention of the Royal Gun Factories was devoted to the question, and their efforts have been crowned with success. First a cheaper iron, sufficiently strong for the exterior of the gun, was obtained; and, secondly, the plan which was proposed by Mr. Fraser, the principal executive officer of the department, was found to be less expensive than the original one.

"Mr. Fraser's plan is an important modification of Sir W. Armstrong's, from which it differs principally in building up a gun with a few long double or triple coils, instead of several short single ones, and a forged breech-piece. There is less material, less labour, and less fine working, and, consequently, less expense, required for the 'Fraser' or present service construction."

Woolwich guns of the Fraser construction only cost about £70 a ton, whilst those built on the original plan cost fully £100 a ton. Nevertheless, the guns thus made are undoubtedly the cheapest, the safest, and best in existence. Even when one or two have been "tested to destruction" it has been found next to impossible to burst them, and, unlike steel or cast iron, they almost invariably give warning. Two of the Frazer guns lie in "The Cemetery" before mentioned, which endured upwards of 2,000 rounds each, with extraordinary charges. before giving way. and the original "Woolwich Infant,"* which is constructed on this system, was fired many times after the experimenters had succeeded in cracking its steel lining, and (with a new "mucous membrane") it is still as good as ever.

STEAM HAMMERS.—There are several steam hammers at work in this forge, but they are of comparatively small power, varying from 30 cwt. to 60 cwt. They are used for welding together short bars of iron, to form the long bar for coiling.

THE PATTERN ROOM.— This repository, sometimes called the "View Room," we reach by passing through the Proof Square, behind the offices. Here are deposited sealed patterns of the guns and fittings manufactured in the Royal Gun Factories, exquisitely finished and tastefully displayed. The warder in charge will, if requested, pass a light down the bore of the muzzle-loading guns to show the beautiful finish of the bore,

---

* The name of the "Woolwich Infant," which has become a household word in all parts of the world, and has been adopted for the whole family of large guns, was suggested to the writer of these pages by Sergeant Major Adamson, of the Depot Brigade, Royal Artillery; and finding its way by that means into print, was universally accepted as the word needed, and has, no doubt, assisted in making the gun famous. (See Frontispiece.)

and the character of the rifling.　This can be seen in breech-loading guns on the removal of the vent-piece, by looking through the piece from breech to muzzle.

The attendant will point out such objects as will interest the visitor.

THE STAINED WINDOW over the north door represents Edward III. and his officers examining an early specimen of brass cannon, and comparing what was then a wonder with an ancient ram, which is seen to the right.　The man on his knees is the founder explaining his handiwork.

This window was removed here in 1874 from the Old Brass Foundry, but, though the subject is antique, the workmanship is probably of the present century.

Passing out of the opposite door and crossing the road obliquely to the left, we enter the

FIELD GUN SECTION (RIFLED ORDNANCE FACTORY.—Here, on the ground floor, we see in various stages of manufacture, the smaller kinds of guns, *i.e.*, field artillery; from the 7-pdr. mountain gun, such as was used in Abyssinia, to the 16-pdr. and 25-pdr.　All the operations of *Boring*, *Turning*, and *Rifling*, seen on a larger scale elsewhere, may be witnessed in this shop.

Here also will be seen the turning of the trunnion arms for light and heavy guns, from the 9-pdr. of 6 cwt. to the 38-ton monster, which could throw a shot of half a ton six miles, or completely over Paris.

Visitors may, if they please, ascend to the upper floors, where the small fittings are made, but, except to mechanical minds, there is no particular feature of interest.

WEST FORGE (OLD FORGE).—Having passed through the Field Gun section, we stand at the broad doorway of this forge, and see before us the

12-*Ton Hammer*.—This was for many years the great hammer of the department, and would be more truthfully described as an 18-ton hammer, for that is the weight of its falling mass. The force of its heaviest blow is computed at 400 tons, while it is under such perfect control that its next blow will crack a nut without wounding the kernel.　At this hammer are produced the large forgings for the trunnion hoops.　The

10-*Ton Hammer* is at the other end of the same forge, and is really a 14-ton hammer. It is used principally for welding the larger coils together, and attaching the trunnion hoops.

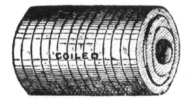 

BORING MILLS.--Recrossing the road, we enter this workshop, and the visitor cannot fail to be struck by the great number and admirable arrangement of its many powerful machines.   The workshop and the marvellous mechanical appliances which it contains may be pronounced perfect specimens of their kind.   On the right are a large number of *Boring Machines,* employed for the most part in boring the A tube* out of the solid steel block, to form the lining of the heavy guns.

As the "cutter" penetrates, a constant stream of water is injected upon it to keep it cool.   The immense pressure required to penetrate the steel would, otherwise, soon reduce the hard steel cutter to as soft a condition as the material it is working upon.

---

* See section of Fraser gun, page 30.

Rifling Machines are here seen at work rifling (*i.e.* cutting the grooves in) the largest descriptions of guns.

This work requires the most watchful care of the attendant, as any hurry or negligence, or even the accidental breaking of a tool, would do serious, if not irreparable damage to the gun.

Vertical Boring Machines.—Two of these powerful machines are seen on the left hand side.

The coils for the superstructure of the larger guns are bored in this workshop, and the breech-pieces are "screwed" to receive the "cascable."

Lapping Machine, near the north door, to rectify any irregularities in the boring.

In the process of boring, the cutter is apt to become a little dull or blunt as it gets near the end of its work, and to make the bore a trifle smaller at the further end. To correct this, and make the bore perfectly parallel, the lapping machine is employed.

The various parts of the gun indicated in our diagram of the Fraser gun, may be traced in all their transition stages about this shop, from the rough forging to the finished article.

THE MUSEUM of the Department is connected with the Boring Mills on the west side, but it is not open to visitors unless provided with a special order. It contains some curious specimens of guns, &c, modern and antique, British and foreign, sections of experimental guns, cut open for inspection, and various other objects of interest, including

The *Testing Machine* in which the whole of the metals used in the construction of guns are thoroughly tried, and their breaking-strength recorded before they are passed into service.

Leaving the Boring Mills by the door at which we entered, we pass on either hand a large collection of monster guns. A very fine display of these guns was arranged on the memorable occasion when the Czar visited the Arsenal.

"*The Infant School*" (see illustration, Page 9) is from a photograph taken on that occasion by the Royal Arsenal Chemical Department. The larger guns are those known in the service as the 35-ton and 38-ton. The others are principally 18-ton and 25-ton guns. All the nations of the earth combined could not have produced another such show.

SHRINKING.—The large hydraulic crane seen in the same sketch is a valuable slave to the great gun makers, lifting with the greatest facility the heaviest guns, and assisting also in the operations of shrinking on the coils, or "building up" the guns. The outer portion is bored somewhat smaller than the portion which it is to encase, but it is expanded by heat and then dropped over it. As it cools (an operation assisted by jets of water) it resumes its original size, and grips the inner coil in its strong embrace—so strong that if the interior were not kept cool by a fountain of cold water within, it would be crushed out of shape.

The experimental gun, which established in a large measure the excellence of the Fraser system, lies among the "school" of guns on the other side of the road. It is a 9-in. muzzle loader, of Fraser construction, without the breech-piece, but reinforced with two double coils, and it has a thin steel lining to the barrel. It was fired, 1,107 times, with a proof projectile of 250 lbs. weight; the first 400 rounds were fired with 30 lbs of powder, the remainder with 43 lb. charges. The steel tube is a little worn by this heavy work, but the gun can still be fired, and if a new tube is inserted it will be rendered serviceable.

THE TURNERIES.—We now enter a building with a handsome front, which contains the turneries where the several parts of the gun are shaped and finished.

It is here that the exact size for all these several parts is obtained with the utmost nicety, in order that one hoop or coil may be shrunk upon another so as to secure perfect solidity without excessive tension. This is one of the scientific elements of gun building, and the care taken to encompass a perfect adjustment of conditions is remarkable.

Powerful Lathes.—In the Turneries we see four magnificent turning lathes. They were made in the department, and are claimed to be superior in power to any such machines in the world. Look in the "beds" beneath them, and you may see the shavings they slice off the solid metal, sometimes 5 inches broad, and forming ringlets of singular beauty. (See Illustration, Page 28.)

Slotting Machine.—Notice also the slotting machine, which removes projections from the rough trunnion hoop, where the lathes cannot get at the surface.

In rear of the turneries are found the

Uniting Furnaces, for joining together the short coils which make the inner tube for cast iron guns converted into rifled guns on the Palliser system.

The two coils, which fit one just within the other, are placed end to end in a furnace, from which the other ends project. When heated to a welding heat, they are squeezed together by passing a bolt through them and screwing it up with a nut. These tubes, after being turned and bored clean, are inserted in the iron guns, which are then rifled as 64-pdrs.

Shrinking and Tempering.—All the smaller guns are here built up, and the "shrinking" is performed as already described.

"Tempering," is toughening the steel tubes, by placing them upright in a furnace heated with wood, lifting them when at the requisite temperature, and plunging them vertically into a bath containing 2,000 gallons of oil, where they remain until cool. By this process the breaking strength of the steel is slightly increased, and (which is more important) its elasticity is largely augmented.

80-ton and 100-ton guns are generally to be seen in the Turneries, where are some of the finest lathes for boring and rifling that were ever made.

THE ROLLING MILLS and PUDDLING FURNACES can now be visited.

The operations performed are, converting cast into malleable iron, and rolling the "blooms" into the required sections or bars for the coils. These things will speak for themselves.

MIGHTY SHEARS.—Close beside the coiling furnace stands a huge "shearing" machine, which will sever bars of iron 7 inches square, with as little apparent effort as though the iron were cheese. The power, however, exerted is so great, that the metal becomes quite hot in the operation.

GROUP OF BOILERS.—A stately group of twenty-four boilers stands close by, for supplying steam to the Steam Hammers and Rolling Mills. These boilers are well worth notice for the manner in which they are arranged, and the complete character and efficiency of their fittings.

THE 40-TON STEAM HAMMER.*—The western-most of the corrugated iron buildings which form the rear range of the Royal Gun Factories, is devoted to the gigantic 40-ton hammer, the most powerful "tool" the world can show. Its falling mass, the "hammer-head," so to speak, weighs exactly 40 tons, and hence its technical description; but its downward force is many times accelerated by its being driven down with steam from the top, a system introduced for the first time on a large scale in this case. It was manufactured by Messrs. Nasmyth and Wilson, of Patricroft, near Manchester, and was fitted up in its present position with such accuracy, that the first time steam was applied to it, the hammer rose and fell as if it had been imbued with life and motion for years.

The foundations beneath the bed of the hammer must, as one may well imagine, be extensive, but few persons would conjecture that they comprise blocks of iron to the weight of six hundred and fifty tons! This, however, is the fact, and the largest block weighs in itself considerably over 100 tons. Besides all this iron, there is timber and concrete to a depth of about 30 feet underground. Two immense fur-

* See Illustration, next page.

THE 40-TON STEAM HAMMER, AND FOUNDATIONS.

naces supply the monster hammer ; and four cranes, whose combined lifting power is above 300 tons, feed it with its food. The large *iron Tongs*, by which the great "heats" are handled, may be seen close by, and as they weigh in themselves about 30 tons, they will afford some idea of the work they have to do. As it is not every day that there is work for the giant, the visitor will be fortunate if he sees it in motion. We cannot do better, therefore, than copy a description of the scene on the occasion of the Czar's visit, in May, 1874, when the hammer was used for the first time :—

"But now the sight of sights is ready. His Majesty passes to the house of the Great Steam Hammer, a large open airy building of corrugated iron and lofty beams, where the Woolwich Titan lives, with all his retinue of furnaces, cranes, cranks, tongs, and pits, and chains, and steam pipes, about him. There has been some dispute as to the pre-eminence of this among all steam hammers. Krupp, at Essen, people say, owns as big a forging tool, and there is a bigger still, somebody avers, in Russia itself. But when it comes to figures, the Woolwich Titan is reinstated. If there be any other hammer which weighs 40 tons, as this does, and is built up of standards, apparatus and anvil containing together over 2,000 tons of solid metal, there is none which has the "back action" in such force. As nearly as percussion can be represented in terms of weight, the stroke of our Titan counts for a thousand tons ! The monster, with a band of swart sons of Vulcan about him, stands, one might say, watching the door of the great furnace by his side, from the chinks of which a red light streams out. Suddenly, up flies the front of the great furnace, disclosing the interior of a burning fiery cave—a chasm of scorching, intense, withering, intolerable incandescence. But, as it cools a little with the outer air, one dimly sees inside the outlines of a vast cylindrical form, slightly, and only slightly, less furiously hot than the seething flame around it. This is a coil for the 38-ton gun, which the sons of Vulcan have got to tackle and carry to the hammer. It weighs 23½ tons. How can they face it ? How can they stir it ? Covered with leathern mail, the swart band goes at the glowing mass with a massive pair of tongs. Lifted by the great crane, they are thrust into the burning fiery furnace. They clasp the trunnion piece round the middle ; they grip it : their grip is riveted upon it by a lever and wedges. Then the crane sways, and the monster lump of blazing iron is dexterously swung under the Titan. There is a little hiss of steam, and down comes the Nasmyth hammer, driving with one terrific blow the loose coils tight, as if that huge red snake made of iron shivered and contracted with pain unspeakable under such a thud. *Cran-n-nch !* but the sound of the impact is intranslatable in any alphabet ! It seems something between a smash of wood, a splash of liquid, and a shattering of metal, as the hammer-head squashes down on the glowing iron, driving squirts of it in red rain all over the building, and driblets of what looks like red hot juice down the coils of the trunnion. How is it that the swarthy craftsmen do not catch fire ? But twenty blows, at the most, have completed the trunnion-piece ; the crane, under the skilful handling of these fireproof Shadrachs of the forge, upsets the forging, and it lies upon its side—a rough, huge, hollow cylinder. The Titan over the anvil is as silent again as a child asleep ; the only sweat upon him is that dribble of red hot iron rain, chilled now into black smuts."

There are two furnaces, one at either end, and the "door" of each contains 1,200 fire bricks, and weighs eight tons. The apparatus by which the doors are lifted is simple and ingenious, consisting of a single long steam cylinder. The door way is large enough to admit an omnibus.

SIGHTING ROOM.—This will complete our journey through the Gun Factories, or it may be omitted. The guns after being built up and rifled, are here vented for "proof," and after passing that ordeal, are fitted with their sights, &c., and finally completed. They are examined carefully by the examining branch of the department, and are then handed over to the custody of the Storekeeper, for the use of the Army and the Navy.

The history of every gun is carefully kept, and every circumstance of note occurring in its manufacture is entered against it, so that, in case of accident or rupture, reference may be made and causes traced.

Throughout this marvellous department, one is struck with the order and system which prevails, as much as by the magnitude and ingenuity of its wonderful mechanisms. To all this perfection of government and mechanical development, the department is greatly indebted to Generals Campbell and Younghusband, and their efficient staff.

For further details respecting the manufactures in the Royal Gun Factories, enquirers are referred to the many excellent works published on modern gunnery, especially the "Treatise on the Construction and Manufacture of Ordnance," by Major J. F. Owen, and Captain Porter, R.A.

ROYAL CARRIAGE DEPARTMENT.

TIMBER FIELD. —The ground covered with logs of timber in rear of the Royal Gun Factories and stretching down by the side of the canal is the Timber Field, and is an appurtenance of the Royal Carriage Department.

We have studied the gun in the Royal Gun Factories, and the Ammunition in the Royal Laboratory, and we now come to examine the appliances by which the gun and the ammunition are rendered efficient by means of the Gun Carriage and its accompaniments.

This is done in the Royal Carriage Department. Formerly, gun carriages were all made of wood, but modern improvements in the gun and ammunition have called for a stronger material, and since 1864, when iron began to replace wood for this purpose, under Colonel Clerk's directions, wood has been gradually superseded, and of late years the Department, under Colonel Field and Colonel Heyman, has developed very rapidly and completely into an important engineering establishment. The gun carriage is now an intricate and highly finished machine, requiring the very best machinery and workmanship for its manufacture.

Wood, however, the original staple of the department, is still largely employed for the manufacture of artillery waggons, military carts, ammunition boxes, ground platforms, and in the repair of the existing wood carriages. We will, therefore, first proceed to

THE SAW MILLS.—The logs being lifted into position by a powerful crane, a gigantic and ingenious cross-cut saw rises through a crevice in the floor, cuts off the rough end neatly, and sinks out of sight again. Two frames, working vertically, and fitted with a number of saws, according to the number and thickness of the planks required, then receive the logs, which run on rollers, and are cut up with "accuracy and despatch."

The cross-cut saw measures 7 feet in diameter, and may be inspected with its mechanism by descending a flight of steps into the vault in which it sleeps. An entertaining description of this saw has been written in *All the Year Round,* by Mr. Wilkie Collins.

MACHINE SHOP.—Adjoining the Frame Shop just described is a large machine-shop, filled with various appliances for manipulating wood, such as

Endless Band Saws,
Circular Saws,
Planing Machines,
Boring Machines,
Wood Lathes,
Special Machines, to produce particular forms in timber and to save hand labour. We direct attention to a very beautiful machine for

Shaping Shafts, which gives the wood the required curve and longitudinal section with wonderful exactness.

WHEELERS AND CARPENTERS' SHOP.—At the back of the Machine Shop will be found this fine workshop, where waggons, ammunition boxes, and various other articles, the character of which the visitor may, if he chooses to remain awhile, determine for himself. But there are wonders yet to see, and, after a short walk in the open air we reach

THE WHEEL FACTORY.—This is one of the most complete establishments of its kind the world contains. The rough timber enters at one door, and after being wholly made by machinery, goes out at another door a perfect wheel.

D

COPYING MACHINES.—By these ingenious machines, invented by Blanchard, an American, almost anything in wood can be carved out, but they are principally used here for

MAKING SPOKES—A mandril of cast-iron is made of the required shape and fixed in the machine. A rough piece of timber is inserted opposite, and is turned out an exact imitation of the cast-iron copy.

The spokes are then buffed at a *glass paper wheel*, which smoothes them to the requisite finish.

They are then removed to another machine, where a revolving cutter *forms the tongue* which has to enter the felloe; and they are now ready to be made up into the wheel.

MAKING FELLOES.—The felloes which form the outer circle of the wheel are *turned* in a special chuck lathe, *planed* at another machine, and *bored* at another to suit the tongues of the spokes, for which they are now ready.

HYDRAULIC PRESS.—Spokes and felloes are taken to a powerful hydraulic press or set of rams, capable of exerting a pressure of 240 tons. The several parts are laid in position on the floor, the rams close in upon them, and spoke and felloe are "squeezed" together into a sound and solid wheel.

SHOEING PIT. The wheel is then removed to a shoeing pit, and the ring tire is shrunk on by being fitted loosely when red hot and sunk in a cold bath, which contracts the iron and grips the whole structure in a firm embrace.

THE NAVES.—These are of the kind known as the "metal Madras naves," and are fitted at a special machine. By this method, all being exactly alike, any nave may at any time be removed and replaced at will.

MOULDING FELLOES. - A special machine may be noted as of a very interesting character. It moulds the edges of the felloes. Like most of the other machinery in the department, it was invented there, and is worth seeing.

ENDLESS SAW AND OSCILLATING TABLE.—This is also in the Wheel Factory. An endless ribband saw revolves round drums, above and below, and the wood which it cuts rests on an iron table or bench, which oscillates in all directions as required, and thus gives to the timber any shape which may be wanted. Some curious specimens of the work it can be made to do are exhibited, but it is chiefly used for cutting bars for saddle trees, which are twisted to a certain curvature to fit the horse's back.

We now leave the Wood, and proceed to the Iron, commencing with

THE MAIN FORGE OR GREAT SMITHERY, a separate building of recent erection, and probably the largest general smith's shop in the kingdom.

There are sixty forges at work, seven or eight steam hammers, ranging from 5 cwt. to 70 cwt., three furnaces, and a very powerful

SHEARING AND PUNCHING MACHINE, by De Bergue, which is worked by a separate engine, and will cut through, or punch a hole in, a sheet of iron $1\frac{1}{2}$ in. thick.

There are also here some of the largest of Ryder's

FORGING MACHINES that have ever been made ; they are used for manufacturing triangular bolts for the naves of wheels, and numerous other articles of that description.

In this shop are forged all the heavier kind of ironwork used in building up gun carriages, such as angle frames for siege carriages, girders for platforms and slides, garrison carriages, &c.

There is also a great deal of *stamping* work done, the hot iron being stamped out in the rough in various forms under the steam hammer.

SCRAP FORGE.—We turn our backs on the great Smithery to enter and pass through the Scrap Forge, where the scrap, or cuttings, of iron are reheated and beaten into shape for use. Here we may see some large

Steam Hammers and

Rolling Mills, for rolling out the iron into bars and bands.

ELEVATION AND PLAN OF GUN CARRIAGE
AND PLATFORM.

A A Trucks for traversing.
b Elevating arc.
c Connecting pin.
d Capstan head.
e Jamming lever.

f Buffer stops.
g Piston of hydr. buffer.
h Hydraulic buffer.
l l Carriage rollers.
n Handspike socket.

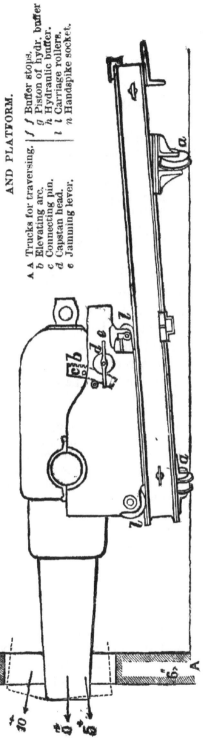

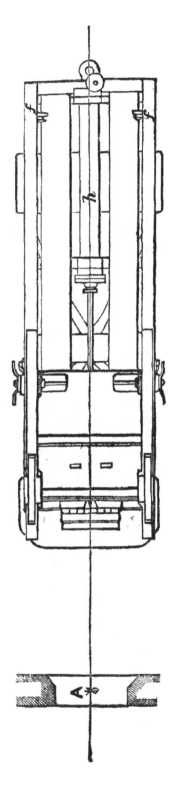

From the Scrap Forge we pass through a door on the left into the

PLATFORM SHOP, which may be described as the EASTERN ANNEXE of the main Factory.

Huge Iron Platforms of various kinds may be seen in various stages of manufacture, the fittings being frequently of an intricate and highly finished character.

These platforms are, generally speaking, used for heavy guns on board ship and in fortifications. Most of the platforms are fitted with hydraulic rams as well as toothed gearing, to assist in working the heavy artillery now in use. The accompanying diagrams represent the elevation and plan of a gun-carriage and platform for land service.

THE MAIN FACTORY, which formerly consisted of a number of workshops, was thrown into one in 1873—9, by Colonels Field and Hayman, assisted by Mr. H. Butter, the Manager of the Department, the change being requisite on account of the stupendous character of the work now to be done, and the consequent necessity for more room.

Machines of the newest and best kinds are here to be seen for preparing the various parts of iron gun-carriages, and for erecting and finishing them.

Travelling Cranes overhead do some of the heaviest work; one in the erecting department being able to lift 20 tons, and another of 12 tons power commands, or rather waits upon, all the heavy machinery in the workshop, being driven by an endless rope and shaft, so that one man, by the use of levers, can lift a complete carriage and platform, and place them in any position required.

The Machinery under the 12-ton crane is of the finest description, comprising some of the best examples of

Planing Machines (duplex and otherwise),

Radial Drilling Machines,

Slotting Machines,

Boring Machines,

Riveting Machines, &c.

The Riveting Machines, for uniting the brackets of the gun-carriages, are very interesting, and should not be passed over.

The west side of the Main Factory is filled with a smaller class of machines, principally lathes for producing parts of the carriages and gear.

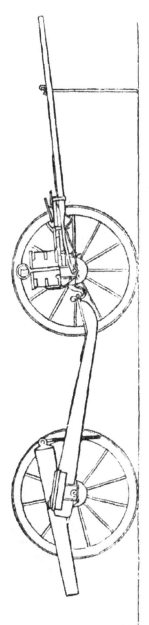

FIELD CARRIAGE SHOP.—

This comprises the WESTERN PORTION of the Main Factory, and here are made the field carriages, limbers, and ammunition waggons, which compose the equipment of the Royal Horse Artillery and Field batteries.

These are made wholly of iron, and it will be well to remark their beautiful structure, graceful contour, exquisite lightness, and remarkable strength   Even non-practical critics will be able to see that the maximum strength is here insured with the minimum of material.   The application of scientific principles in the construction of gun carriages has of late years added largely to the power of our artillery, and the result reflects the highest credit on the Superintendent, and the constructional skill of his subordinate officers.

Endless Band Saw for Cutting Iron.—This delicate looking, but really powerful machine may be seen in this and several other workshops.   It was, like many other appliances here witnessed, an invention of the department, and is now generally used in engineering shops throughout the kingdom.   It will saw through iron of any thickness, and shape it in any form required—a marvellous improvement on the old " drilling and chipping" process.   The

SMITH'S SHOPS contain some

machinery for forging bolts, nuts, and rivets.

These shops also contain the largest assortment of stamping tools to be found in any factory in the kingdom.   There are stamps for shaping the hot iron under the steamhammer into all the lighter and most intricate forgings connected with field carriages.

BOLT AND NUT MAKING.—The visitor may pass into a shop for Finishing and Screwing all kinds of bolts and nuts required in the manufactures of the department.

PATTERN ROOM. — Passing out of the main block, and leaving on the left a range of buildings which contain the more perishable stores in the raw material, the visitor will see a structure of large and imposing appearance. This is the Pattern Room of the Royal Carriage Department, and it contains highly finished specimens of the general manufactures of the Department.

An inspection of the carriages, &c., here exhibited, cannot fail to interest the spectator and afford a good general idea of the excellence of the workmanship exercised in their production.

It may here be stated that the numerous and intricate fittings are all gauged, or measured, with the nicest accuracy, by a staff of skilled examiners, by which means all the parts are interchangeable, and the detection of any unsound material or defective workmanship is secured.

An enumeration of the articles here contained would be a general description of all the war material used in the service, which may be studied in Major Kemmis's book on "Carriage Department Stores." Sufficient for the general reader will be explained by the intelligent custodian in charge of the museum, and the visitor will see some curiosities in the galleries, including

A Bird's Nest in the trunk of a tree. This was found in the Department while some men were cutting a log of elm timber in 1863. When the log was sawn in two, a hole was discovered running longitudinally up the trunk. After removing a quantity of hay and other light substances, a well formed nest was seen, containing three eggs, one of which was broken in the sawing. From the size of the log and the central position of the nest, it is supposed to have been enclosed for a hundred years. The hole lies in the direction of the grain, and was so perfectly enclosed by sound wood, that there is no trace of its existence beyond an inch each way, which is a little decayed. To add to the curiosity, the eggs are not of the same kind, one being laid by a sparrow, and the other by a tom-tit.

Indian Ants. — An example of the destruction worked by these industrious, but mischievous, insects is also exhibited. They consume in a few hours all the vegetable tissue of any wooden article exposed to their ravages, and leave a beautiful skeleton of itself, fit to crumble at a touch.

This completes the TOUR OF THE ROYAL ARSENAL. It should be observed, however, that the route is sometimes reversed.

APPENDIX TO THE ROYAL ARSENAL.

THE EAST LABORATORY.—Divided from the rest
of the Royal Arsenal by high walls or by water, and inaccessible to strangers unless provided with special authority is the East Laboratory or Composition Department, where the small arm cartridges are made; further a-field, in the Marsh-land on the other side of the Canal, are the rocket factories and detonating sheds; while remoter still, down the river bank, is the Cannon-Cartridge Factory. Hundreds of boys and a few men are employed in these dangerous operations, and so perfect is the system on which they are conducted, that accidents are very rare. Major Majendie, Her Majesty's Inspector of Gunpowder Factories, and formerly Assistant Superintendent of the Laboratory Department, has brought all his intellectual experience to bear in making this the model of its kind; and so many improvements have been effected here of late years that it may safely be said there is no establishment in existence so perfect. Still accidents do occur, and it is believed that they always will occur, in spite of every precaution. Machinery has been devised, by which risky operations are performed in a tube, through which the force of an accidental explosion is carried harmlessly away, and ingenious contrivances have been devised, by which the "life" of the cartridge (as we may call its detonating arrangement) is attached to it at the very last moment; but, for all these safeguards, an unsuspected grain of sand or grit of iron may create a spark, and terrible consequences unforeseen accrue. Everybody employed in these works changes his clothes on entering, so as to avoid the possibility of taking in a lucifer match or other dangerous article; and everybody puts on boots in which there are no nails but copper ones. Large slippers, in which persons entering the enclosures on business encase their feet, are also provided, and

any visitor permitted to enter will gain some idea of " snow-shoe" travelling.

The gunpowder and the manufactured ammunition are stored in two large magazines some distance away down the marshes, and on barges and hulks in the river.

THE CARTRIDGE CASE FACTORY, in which also a number of boys are employed, is a large and commodious building, just inside the Marsh Gate. On account of its distance from the other parts of the Arsenal, it is seldom troubled with strangers ; but the handy little machines and the busy little workers are well worth a visit.

THE SALE YARD is adjacent to the last mentioned factory, and it is here that the old stores are collected and sold by auction at periodical dates, on which occasions there is a considerable immigration from the regions of Hounsditch.

THE INNER PRACTICE RANGE, as the open ground commencing at the Sale Yard is termed, is about a mile long, but is only used now for short ranges, up to 500 yards, as there is a longer range outside the Arsenal. It is here that the various kinds of rifles and ammunition are tested. Being fired from a fixed rest at the immense iron targets which stand at the north end, a record is kept of a succession of shots. If from the same fixed point the rifle registers its shots close together on the target—say twenty hits within the size of a dinner plate—it is considered to have made a " good diagram," and the rifle, or the ammunition, whichever is being tried, is credited accordingly. It is obvious that a rifle or cartridge which does not shoot straight, when properly directed, is not to be trusted.

THE TORPEDO RANGE is a long reach of the canal in which the fish torpedoes make their trial trips or " runs."

THE BALLOON GROUND, from whence aerial ascents are made for military and scientific purposes, is just beyond the canal, which visitors are forbidden to cross except by special permission.

THE PROOF BUTTS.—Close to the targets aforesaid, are the Proof Butts, at which the great guns are tested. The butts are high mounds of earth faced with baulks of timber, and " pierced " with bays or sand holes, into which the guns are fired. Every gun intended for the service has to stand a certain

number of rounds with the proof charge, which is generally about
one-fifth heavier than the service charge.   When "proved to
destruction," just to see what they can endure, the guns are
crammed half full of powder, and jammed up with a great bolt
of iron sticking a foot or two out of the muzzle.   For the security
of the range party, the guns are fired by electricity from a safe
position under cover.   They were formerly fired by slow burning fuzes, which enabled the men to reach a safe distance before
the discharge took place; but a rather remarkable accident occurred in the month of February, 1852, which led to a modification of the system then in use, and the ultimate adoption of the
present plan.   Several large guns were lying side by side, loaded
and pointed to the butts.   The first which was fired burst, and
one of its fragments struck the next gun, causing it to "wheel"
round in the direction of the town.   When its charge ignited,
the shot flew into the air over the Arsenal and the streets of
Woolwich, where it was seen and heard whizzing overhead,
and finally descended, two miles away, through the roof and
several floors of a house in the Dockyard, close to the gates.   As
it was just the dinner hour, some thousands of workmen were
crowding out of the gates, and it was almost miraculous that
no one was injured.

It is somewhat remarkable that there should have been a
similar occurrence at the Arsenal more than a hundred years
before.   In 1742, an old newspaper says:—

"On Friday there was a proof of iron ordnance at Woolwich,
when a 24 pdr. burst, and a piece of metal of about 4 cwt. flew near
300 yards over the heads of the people, and fell upon the top of a
chimney of a house adjoining the founder's, broke through the roof
and through three stories down to the ground floor, and providentially
did no other mischief.   The gun in its agitation before bursting,
turned that which lay next to it so as to point its muzzle towards the
spectators and the storekeeper's house, and had it not struck out the
portfire, which was lighted, great mischief would probably have
ensued."

Accidents, however, seldom occur at the Proof Butts, but
there was once an occurrence which might have had tragical, but
fortunately had only farcical, consequences.   Among the thousands of "inventions" which have here been tested, too often to
their failure, was a light gun proposed to be mounted on a mule's
back, and fired from thence, much as a ship's stern-chaser delivers her fire at the pursuing foe.   A great deal of interest,

though little faith, was felt in this new plan of field artillery, and a number of officers assembled to witness the trial. A mule not being readily procurable, a gentle donkey was pressed into the service, and bore the process of lashing on the gun and loading with powder and ball as meekly and as unconcernedly as is his kindred's wont. It was thought advisable for the spectators to retire a few paces in order to observe the effect of the recoil, and a slow match being lit, the quadruped was left standing alone. Great was the astonishment and alarm of the " committee" when poor Neddy, overjoyed at his unaccustomed liberty, began to move and caper about, changing front by wheeling on the centre, and sweeping the horizon with the muzzle of his gun, apparently choosing some object to aim at. The experimenters, not desiring to offer themselves a sacrifice to science in such an ignominious fashion, sought cover where they could, or threw themselves flat on mother earth, and when the loud report told that the danger was past, every one was delighted to find himself unhurt. All that we can record relative to the result of the experiment, is that the shock was too much for the donkey, for he was rolled over, head-first, several yards away, but where the shot went has never been discovered. This is the story ; for its complete accuracy we are not able to vouch.

CONVICTS' GRAVES.—Behind the butt and close inside the river wall may be discerned a row of hillocks which mark the spot where the unhappy prisoners who died in the hulks were buried. There used to be some hundreds of these graves scattered about various parts of the Arsenal, and the remains of the bodies have frequently been found in excavating for modern buildings. They were buried in rough boxes or coffins, and some of their skeleton forms have been discovered *in irons*—their fetters being buried with them to augment the ignominy of their disgraceful end; others of the coffins have been found quite empty, the corpses having either been abstracted by " body-snatchers," or appropriated before leaving the hulks for "study," the human form divine being in great request for such purposes fifty years ago.

THE OUTER RANGE, beyond the Arsenal wall, is where practice is carried on both with small arms and heavy ordnance. It is much used by the volunteers from London, for whom special facilities are afforded.

THE GAS WORKS are near the canal on the west side. They supply not only the Royal Arsenal, but the Barracks, Dockyard, and all the Government buildings, and have been in operation since about the year 1857. Previous to that time, the public works were supplied by the two local Gas Companies. The Government, by making its own gas, saves wharfage and some other expenses, besides getting the advantage arising from large orders and extended contracts with the colliery owners, and it has some special facilities for cheap manufacture not possessed by the gas companies. Taking all this into consideration, it is not surprising that we here find the gas made at the minimum of cost. There are several large gasometers at these works, the most capacious holding 100,000 feet. To ascertain how much the gasometer contains, count the number of rings or divisions which are to be seen above ground; each division contains 10,000 feet. In the middle of the works is a large grass plot, from which scientific balloon ascents are sometimes made. In 1874, the chimney shaft, which had sunk 4 feet out of the perpendicular, was straightened by sawing a wedge-piece out of one side.

THE GUN GROUNDS in rear of the Gas Works and beyond the Canal Bridge are covered with thousands of large guns, many of cast-iron. English guns, as elsewhere explained, are seldom made of cast-iron now-a-days, and these were all made by contract, principally at the north country ironworks. Now that the old system is universally condemned, it is something for the Royal Gun Factories to boast of, that it never made a cast-iron gun which went on service, which we believe to be the fact; but these old guns deserve to be respected, for it was with them and their fellows that the great naval battles which have established England's supremacy on the waves have been fought. Rabbits, no doubt the descendants of those who a century or two ago flourished in the " Warren," are occasionally to be seen sporting about, in and out these old cannon, beneath which they have their burrows. Behind the Gas Works is the spot where formerly stood the butts, and guns were proved there as late as 1851. There was a swamp around it famed for snipe, but the mound and the swamp have long since been made level, and the snipe have migrated to the marshes beyond.

CURIOUS GUNS.—At the north edge of the gun ground by the roadside near the Proof Offices, is a collection of guns, each of which has a history. There is one which bears the following record :—

"This gun was on board H.M.S. "Orion," at the Battle of Trafalgar. In the year 1850 it was on board H.M.S. "Reynard," when wrecked on the Prata Shoal, in the China Seas ; and in 1860 it was found in the Taku Forts, when captured by the Allied Armies."

Behind the Weigh Bridge Office lie the fragments of old wrought iron guns, recovered in 1836, from the wreck of the "Mary Rose," which was sunk off Spithead in the reign of Henry the Eighth, A.D., 1545. The remains are much corroded and damaged, but they are interesting as specimens of wrought iron ordnance made so long ago.

HOLIDAYS IN THE ARSENAL.—The Royal Arsenal is closed, and a free holiday given to the officials and work people on Christmas Day and Good Friday, the birthday of the ruling Sovereign, and Coronation Day. But the holiday which they probably esteem more than any other is that on the second Saturday in July, which is a special and extra holiday, known as "Bean-feast Day," and is usually spent in excursions to some country place and a dinner, at which beans form an indispensable dish. The general tradition and belief is that this holiday has a royal origin, but opinions differ as to the date when it commenced and the monarch by whom it was given, while some few have the heresy to declare that it is no more than a mere workshop custom, such as is found to prevail in most of the large industrial establishments throughout the kingdom. Our own belief is that the holiday, if not the name it bears, was instituted by King George the Third, when he visited the Arsenal on July 9th, 1772, and feasted at the Academy.* The date being in the second week of July is remarkable (though it appears to have fallen on a Tuesday instead of a Saturday), and a gentleman formerly connected with the Royal Laboratory informs us that some twenty years ago he saw, among some ancient lumber at the old offices, a book containing the veritable manuscript order, expressing the King's admiration of the wonderful skill of his workmen, and giving them a day for their enjoyment in all perpetuity. It is reported that the King had beans at his table in the Aca-

---

* See " History of Royal Arsenal."

demy, which is likely enough, as they were probably in season in July, and that he made it a condition of his gracious indulgence that the workmen should eat beans at all future anniversaries, which seems absurd. "Bean-feasts" were old English institutions long before "George the Third was king," and it is more reasonable to suppose that the name, being ready to hand, was made use of, than that it should have had such a doubtful and out of the way origin.

SOUTH ARCH OF THE ROYAL ARTILLERY BARRACKS,
WOOLWICH.

WOOLWICH GARRISON.

If the visitor would see more of Woolwich after leaving the Royal Arsenal, he should proceed by way of Green's End and New Road, towards the Common. In New Road he will pass the

LOWER BARRACKS,

an unpretentious building, which was formerly the head-quarters of the Royal Engineers, then called the Royal Sappers and Miners, before the staff of the regiment was removed to Chatham. It was for some time afterwards used as quarters for the practical class of Cadets from the Royal Military Academy, but has now been handed over to the Royal Artillery, though it is still partly occupied by a few of the red-coated Engineers, the men of the scientific corps who conduct our siege operations in times of war, and map out our country, construct our telegraphs, and build our bridges, in the " piping times of peace." No man is admitted into the corps of Engineers who has not a trade in his hands and a good character at his back. The men are consequently of a superior class.

Passing the Roman Catholic and Scotch Churches and the High School, we see on the left an extensive block of buildings which are now the

ARMY SERVICE CORPS BARRACKS.

This building was partially erected in 1780, and opened as a soldiers' hospital. An old newspaper, under date of April 8th, in that year says: " The new hospital opened on Monday last, at Woolwich Common, for the reception of patients, is calculated to hold 200 beds." In 1806, it was enlarged by the addition of buildings " to accommodate 700 men." It was used as a hospital until the Herbert Hospital, at Shooters' Hill, was opened, when it was converted into barracks for the Military Train, now the Army Service Corps. This Corps, though regarded as non-combatants, and intended to do the *carving* and *carrying* for the army, are a really smart body of soldiers, fairly drilled and well instructed in military duties, notwithstanding that the bulk of their time is employed in various kinds of labour at the Royal Arsenal, where the officers and non-commissioned officers are engaged in the offices, and the men are employed at workshops, stores and wharves. This most useful branch of the Army is composed of two parts—"the Ordnance" and "the Transport," the former being such as attend to the food, clothing, and other necessaries for the army, while the latter convey the stores and other *impedimenta* from place to place, as required. The corps is now organized on a system which experience has made nearly perfect. Opposite this building, on our right hand, are

THE DEPOT BARRACKS.

The main block of these barracks was built and opened as " The Military Clothing Store," the remainder, now stables, being called " The Grand Depot," as the bulk of England's Artillery was here deposited. The Clothing Store was removed to the larger establishment of the kind at Pimlico, in 1868, and after the building had been used as a mere store for some years, it was made over to the Commandant of the Garrison, and transformed into barracks for the Royal Artillery, in connection with the great Barracks we shall presently see. A little farther on the Riding School (153 feet by 63 feet) and *Menages* are disclosed, where the troops learn their riding and sword exercises; and next appears a plain but handsome building,

The Royal Artillery Institution.

To this building, we need not say, ordinary visitors have no entry. It is intended solely for the instruction and amusement of the officers of the Royal Artillery, many of whom, by taking advantage of the facilities it affords, continue their studies here long after leaving the Academy, to shine out afterwards among the brilliant warriors and scientific scholars for which the Royal Regiment of Artillery is distinguished. The Institution has a commodious theatre or lecture room, a printing office, a photographic studio, a very fine museum, and other luxuries; and an observatory on the other side of the Barrack Field, fitted with a very powerful telescope, erected a few years ago, at a cost of more than £500. It is entirely supported by the subscriptions of its members, among whom are nearly all the officers of the regiment, some 1,500 in number, some officers of kindred corps, and other men of science. The building was erected in 1854, and the front is uniform with that of the Riding School, after the model of an ancient temple.

The Royal Artillery Barracks.

whose extensive and imposing front we next see facing the broad green common, is one of the finest buildings of its kind in England. It is built in the form of a parallelogram, and may be described as consisting of six ranges of brick buildings, each more than 400 feet in length. At first, the barracks, when erected in 1775, consisted only of the eastern half of the present building. Early in the present century its capacity had to be doubled to meet the growth of the royal regiment, and the architect by a simple rule of multiplication, took ground to the right, and built a corresponding block, uniting the two with Doric arches front and back, which gives to the whole edifice a completeness and uniformity of design as perfect as though the whole building had been drawn in the original plan. The central arch facing the common is surmounted with the royal arms and military trophies, and the east and west gates respectively bear coats of arms, which fix the dates of the two wings. The former bears the arms of the Duke of Richmond, Master General in 1775; and the latter the arms of the Earl of Chatham, Master General in 1806. The front is further divided by four handsome intervals of masonry in the brickwork, with stone columns supporting the *fascia*. These intervals, taking them in rotation are *the Garrison Recreation Rooms, the Guard Room, the Officers' Mess,* and *the Commandant's Offices*. The theatre at the Recreation Rooms has a really beautiful interior. It was originally the garrison church, and was converted to its present use when the curch opposite was erected in 1863, after being kept closed for a year or so, in order that its sanctity might grow cold. It will accommodate nearly 1,500 persons, and is used principally for giving dramatic entertainments to the soldiers, at which the performers are generally the officers and non-commissioned officers of the garrison. There are also in the same building, rooms for reading, smoking, refreshments, and various kinds of games, including a *bona fide* skittle alley. The Guard-rooms and Offices need no description, but of the Officers' Mess Room it may be said that it is one of the noblest in existence. It has in connection with it a valuable and extensive library of 40,000 volumes, a reading room, billiard rooms, &c., and the upper floors are approached by a staircase of magnificent proportions. There is scarcely a crowned sovereign, or person of high distinction who has figured in Europe during the last half century, but has been entertained at the mess-room of the Royal Artillery, which is everywhere renowned for its wealth and grandeur, and its princely hospitality. Its store of plate is exceedingly rich, and comprises gifts from kings and emperors, souvenirs from other regiments, and spoils taken from the enemy, one of the recent additions being a massive ram's head of unalloyed gold, captured at the palace of the barbarous Ashantee King.

The Crimean Memorial,

which faces the south arch of the Royal Artillery Barracks, from the other side of the grand parade, is a bronze statue of Victory, as in the act of crowning her warriors with wreaths of laurel. It was erected to the memory of the officers and men of the Royal Artillery who fell in the Crimea during the Russian War of 1854-6, and it was cast out of cannon captured from the enemy.   The high pedestal upon which it is erected, bears the following inscription on its front.—

"HONOUR TO THE DUTIFUL AND BRAVE."

On a shield in rear it is stated that the statue was—

"Erected by their Comrades, to the Memory of the
Officers, Non-Commissioned Officers, and Men
of the Royal Regiment of Artillery,
who fell during the War with Russia, in the years
1854, 1855, and 1856."

THE GREAT GUN FROM BHURTPORE

stands in rear of the Crimean statue.   This trophy was captured at the fortress of Bhurtpore, and was entrusted by King George IV., in 1828, to the care of the Royal Artillery and Royal Engineers, as a special mark of His Majesty's approbation of their services, with directions that it should be mounted in front of the Barracks at Woolwich.*   The gun is 16 feet 4 inches in length, and weighs 17¾ tons.   The diameter of the bore, or calibre, is 8 inches, and it is supposed to have been made by the Mogul Emperor Aurangzeb, so long ago as 1677. It was long imagined that the gun contained in its composition a large quantity of gold and silver, but Professor Able, the War Department Chemist, has proved that this is a delusion.   The metal is principally copper, but contains some 10 per cent. of lead and 4 per cent. of tin.   The exterior of the breech is, however, of brass, cast over the gun after its otherwise completion.   The inscriptions upon the gun are Mahomedan attributes of the great Aurangzeb and his glorious ancestors.

There are also on the Royal Artillery parade ground

FOUR FLORENTINE GUNS.

precisely alike, except for their names, inscribed on a scroll, which are "Violentum," "Testudo," "Destructor," and "Negans."

ST. GEORGE'S CHURCH.

This beautiful edifice, incomplete as it seems without tower or spire, commands admiration for its magnificent proportions, its elegant design, and perfect workmanship.   But it is the internal rather than the external aspect which most impresses the be-

---

* A full description of this gun is given in the *Official Catalogue* of the Rotunda.

holder—the vast space enclosed within the walls, its lofty elevation, its chancel broad and deep, its noble stone pulpit and marble
reading desks, its many stained glass windows, and its massive
character in every part, all tending to a feeling of awe and
reverence and devotion.   The stained glass windows are all
memorials to officers connected with the garrison, and have been
presented by relatives, comrades, and friends.   That over the
principal entrance is in memory of Lord Sydney Herbert, of
Lea, the Secretary of State for War who supervised the erection
of the church, and after whom the Herbert Hospital, which may
be called one of his greatest works, is named.   The church,
which was opened, in November, 1863, belongs to the nation,
and its clergy are chaplains in the army ; it has a very fine organ
and a splendid choir, most of the singers being members of the
Royal Artillery Band, which, it need not be said, is unsurpassed,
not only in England, but probably throughout the world.   If we
are apt to deal a little too freely with superlatives at Woolwich,
it is not in relation to the Royal Artillery Band that we are in
any danger of being confounded.

The Officers' Cricket Ground

on the Barrack Field may be mentioned.   Great care is taken
to preserve its condition ; and some grand matches are played
here during the season.   Other cricket-grounds for the non-
commissioned officers and soldiers of the Garrison are formed
on the further side of the Barrack Field, towards the

Royal Military Repository.

The Repository is on the western side of the Barrack Field,
enclosed within an earthwork fortification, through whose embrasures, and above whose parapets, the great guns may be seen
with which the young soldiers take what are called their
" Repository exercises," which embrace the mounting and dis-
mounting of heavy ordnance, lifting and moving heavy weights
by various mechanical appliances, pontooning on the lake, and
all the variety of services which our gunners have to perform in
our forts and garrisons at home and abroad.   All officers of
Artillery, including those of the Militia and Volunteers, have to
pass a term of instruction here for a month or more, and the
term of probation is called " school."   Within the Repository
enclosure, but approached by a separate entrance, is that well-

known museum of military history and science, the Rotunda, to which we shall presently come.

The Garrison Female Hospital

for soldiers' wives and children, is a modest building retiring behind what is known as the Auxiliary Hospital, near the

EXTERIOR OF FEMALE HOSPITAL

White Gate. It is a little model of its kind, and does a most useful work; and we call attention to it, not so much for the purpose of attracting visitors, though they (ladies especially) will always be welcome, as to advocate the claim it has upon those who have the means and the disposition to help works of charity, for it is mainly supported by voluntary subscriptions.

INTERIOR OF FEMALE HOSPITAL.

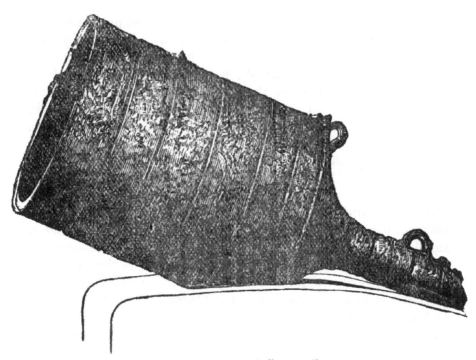

AN ANCIENT "GONNE"

Exhibited at the Rotunda, Woolwich, one of the earliest guns known to exist. It was found in the Moat at Bodiham Castle, and probably dates from about 1350.

THE ROTUNDA.

This famous museum is *open free every day* (except Sunday) from 10 till 6 in Summer, and from 10 till 4 in Winter, and forms a striking object on the landscape, from its spacious dimensions, its circular form, and its high pagoda-like roof The *Official Catalogue*, to which we refer the visitor for full information, both as to the Rotunda and its contents, and many other facts of interest, states that the building was originally erected in St. James's Park, for the reception of the Allied Sovereigns on their visit to England in 1814. Its original position may be seen upon a curious model which is exhibited inside, representing the park as it then existed, with the various triumphal and festal buildings erected in honour of that memorable event. The Rotunda is 116 feet in diameter, and covers an area of 10,600 square feet, being very nearly two-thirds as large as Westminster

Hall. The central pillar, by which the roof is at present in part supported, is a comparatively recent addition. As originally constructed, and for several years after its removal to Woolwich, the roof was entirely self-sustained ; nothing prevented the eye from taking in the full extent of the surface covered. To this building, after its erection on the present site, were transferred, in 1820, the objects which the great fire of 1802 had spared of the original contents of the Repository founded in the Arsenal in 1778, by Captain William Congreve, R.A., afterwards highly distinguished as Lieut. General Sir W. Congreve. The museum abounds with records of the fertile invention of Sir W. Congreve, and his equally remarkable son. To the original collection as thus constituted, the Prince Regent was pleased to transfer a small but valuable collection of mediæval arms and armour ; and finally, since the transfer of the establishment by the late Lord Herbert, of Lea, from the custody of the Commandant of the Garrison of Woolwich to that of the Ordnance Select Committee in 1859, the liberality of the Government has permitted several purchases of arms and models, as well as the deposition of a great variety of objects which have already passed out of the service, or are in danger of doing so at an early date. To some extent it is, in fact, a museum of the future, aiming to preserve for another generation of artillerymen much that would be otherwise swept away by the tide of change.[*]

It is not within the scope or intention of this work to give anything like a description of the many thousand remarkable things to be seen in this wonderful museum —the catalogue, which is published by authority, and is most exact and accurate, can alone do that. It can be purchased in the Rotunda. The attendants, military and civil, are also invariably intelligent and courteous to visitors, and will point out and explain the objects of greatest interest. As, however, the reader may not have either catalogue or guide, we will endeavour to point out the way in which he may best make a tour of the museum, so as to take in the whole of the exhibition.

OUTSIDE are seen guns of various dates and nationalities, including several from China ; and a Chinese gun-carriage as barbarous in its construction as their guns are artistic. The large bronze cannon in two parts, screwing together, was brought

---

[*] General Lefroy's Introduction to 1864 Edition of Official Catalogue.

from the Dardanelles in 1648. It fired the stone shot lying adjacent.

The *Iron Targets* which stand about the doorway of the building are worthy of notice. They represent the iron plates with which various ships are armed, and they show the effects wrought upon them by the hard-headed shot and shell with which they have been battered for experiment. The Palliser and other shells which have done all this mischief lie close by, and the little injury which their sharp noses have received in the contact is astonishing.

INSIDE, we should *pause* for a moment to take a general survey, and endeavour to master the plan of the exhibition, which, from its circular arrangement, is apt to deceive.

FIRE ARROW, A.D. 1650.

TURN TO THE RIGHT, and we take a glance on either side of the avenue as we pass along. Then we shall see

On the *Left* hand—Models of Plymouth and Sheerness Dockyards.

On the *Right*—Ancient stone shot and modern shell.

Stands of small arms arranged against all the side pillars. Every rifle in existence, including the breech-loaders of every nation in Europe, is here represented.

On the *Left*—Model of the City and Harbour of Rio Janeiro.

On the *Right*—Models of a Rocket Train and Rocket Apparatus. The curious doll in a cage illustrates a plan suggested by Colonel Congreve for saving life from wrecks.

Native Australian weapons against the wall.

On the *Left*—Case of Arms and Incendiary and Explosive Projectiles, Ancient and Modern, from the old fire-arrow*, and hand grenade of rough glass, to the most improved shells of the present day.

Models of the British Artillery occupy the summit of this case.

A wonderful Cinder is generally kept in this case. It is all that was left when the old £1 notes were destroyed. Notes to the value of £100,000 were burnt in a stove, and this is the *cinder*.

On the *Right*—Model of old fashioned Machine for Venting Guns, and models showing the method of making Charcoal for Gunpowder.

Native weapons of Polynesia on the walls.

On the *Left*—Model of Chatham Dockyard, and model of an old Cannon Foundry.

Model of Portsmouth Dockyard.

Model of the Citadel of Brimstone Hill.

Laboratory Products : a fine case of specimens of Warlike Stores, beautifully arranged.

Case of Sights, Tangent Scales, and implements.

Behind this, model of the Ballistic Pendulum for calculating the initial velocity of shot.

Case showing specimens of Gunpowder. Note the "Pebble" Powder, with "grains" as large as walnuts.

On the *Right*—Against the wall : native weapons of South Africa. Ancient Spears, &c.

On the *Left* - Case of Gun Locks, &c.

Behind it—Naval Models : one illustrates the mode of shipping horses. See model of an ancient Bomb-ship, with the incipient turret of to-day ; also an ancient "First-rater."

A magnificent model of Gibraltar, 36 feet in length, admirably executed. Another model of Gibraltar is in rear of this.

On the *Right*—A case containing trophies of the compaign in Abyssinia, and other curiosities.

In a recessed apartment on the right hand—a French brass 12-pr. field gun and equipment, presented by the late Emperor Napoleon III., in 1858. One of the English field-guns and equipment were presented to the Emperor by Queen Victoria in return.

Small arms, mostly modern, appear on the walls of this recess.

A long gun in the centre is a *Faulconneau* of the seventeenth century, on a swivel carriage. There is also a long forged field-gun of the 17th century.

---

* See Illustration, Page 64.

At the *entrance* of the recess, on a pedestal, is a curious instrument for measuring time. It is said to be the nearest approach to "perpetual motion" yet discovered.

On the *Right*—Case of Ancient Armour and Weapons.

On the *Left*—Model of St. James's Park, showing the position of the Rotunda at the Peace rejoicings in 1814.

Case of swords, ancient and modern.

Model to represent dispersion of shell bursting in flight.

Case of Swords—Dress and duelling.

Model of the King's Bastion, Gibraltar.

On the *Right* - Chinese flags, shields, weapons, dresses, and paraphernalia of war.

Scythe infernal machine.

Chinese and Japanese saddles.

A curious trophy of relicts from the fire in the Tower of London, on October 30th, 1841.

Case illustrative of shells and fuzes.

On the *Left*—Great model of Quebec.

Model illustrating different modes of crossing chasms in India, &c.

Model of Landport Gate, Portsmouth ; and behind, a Pontoon bridge.

On the *Right*—Tomahawks and other North American Indian weapons, snow shoes, &c.

On the Table—set of models, 22 in number, of a battery of Russian Artillery. This very interesting group was presented by the Czar to the Duke of Wellington in 1834.

A wooden cannon.

On the *Left*—Model of a Maximilian Tower in Austria.

Breech-loading Gun recovered from the "Mary Rose," sunk in 1545.

This completes the circuit and brings us to the *Entrance* again.

Proceeding *towards the centre column* of the building, we pass a number of guns, every one of which has a history. The most interesting is probably

No. 1—1 in the Catalogue, an ancient "gonne,"* probably of the 14th century. This is one of the earliest guns known to exist, and it was used for throwing stone balls, specimens of which are exhibited close by. It was found in the moat at Bodiham Castle, and was for many years exhibited at Battle Abbey.

Distributed about the central space we find

A large model of Torres Vedras.

A fine model of the Island of St. Helena, showing the spot where Napoleon lived and died in exile, and the place of his tomb.

A model on larger scale of Buttermilk Point, St. Helena.

A valuable case of flint implements, of remote antiquity.

Several ancient guns, hand mortars, &c., including that illustrated on next page.

---

* See Illustration, page 67.

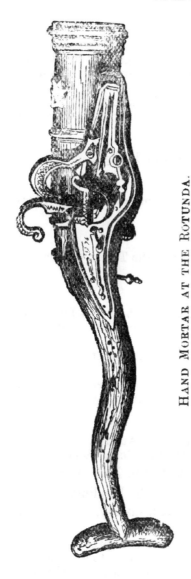

HAND MORTAR AT THE ROTUNDA.

Vertical sections, showing the armour-plating of various iron-clad ships.

A case of flint arrow heads, &c.

Rifles of various kinds surrounding the central pillar, the peculiarities of which must be exhibited and explained to be understood.

Rifle batteries of many barrels. One of these "infernal machines" has 31 barrels, all of which are fired by one percussion cap at a single pull of the trigger.

The Prussian system of breech-loading guns, illustrated by a 12-pdr. (Krupp's) steel gun, and the breech arrangement of a 100-pdr. on the same plan, slightly modified. This is probably the simplest method of breech-loading, though it will be seen partly developed in some of the ancient models close to it.

The Armstrong breech-loader shows the plan adopted by England for the short period breech-loading guns were in fashion.

An old English breech-loading gun, date 1483. The breech end lifts out to be charged, and there is a duplicate breech to save time in loading. The forging is rude, and was apparently executed at some ancient smithy.

In the old breech-loading guns here shown, we see the germ of nearly all the designs of our present day. "There is nothing new under the sun."

A large model of the Crimea, showing Sebastopol, Balaclava, and the famous Battle fields.

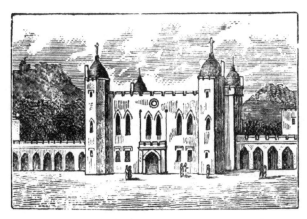

QUADRANGLE OF THE ROYAL MILITARY ACADEMY,
BURNT AND RESTORED, 1873.

THE ROYAL MILITARY ACADEMY

is about a mile from the Royal Arsenal Gates, on a part of Woolwich Common, to the left of the road leading to Eltham. It was built about the year 1801, from a design by Sir J. Wyatville, in castellated form. In the front centre is a handsome quadrangular elevation with a minaretted tower at each corner. This contains the Library, Reading Room, the Offices of the Governor and Secretary, and one or two class rooms and studies. From either side of this quadrangle, arched corridors communicate with the cadets' quarters in the wings, to which, at either end, a new block has been added in recent years. There is a fine dining hall in the centre enclosure, with some historic paintings and trophies of arms on the walls, and the rear is occupied by cookhouses and other offices. Further beyond, detached from the Academy building, and of recent erection, are Billiard Rooms, Workshops for the Cadets, and a magnificent School of Arms or Gymnasium. With few exceptions, all the young officers appointed to the " scientific corps"—as the Royal Artillery and Royal Engineers are termed—have had to pass through this academy, being previously prepared at private schools, of which there are several good examples at Woolwich.* While at the

* Charles Knight traces the remote origin of the Academy to a private school which existed at Charlton before 1719, the precursor also of the many military schools of the present day.

Academy, a large sum has to be paid for their maintenance and education, but they are granted by the Government a liberal allowance of pocket money. They are generally at the Academy about two years, and are under strict discipline, any breach of which subjects the offender to "rustication" for a term (which means sending him home for six months), or even dismissal. The worst offence a Gentleman Cadet can commit is to tell a lie.

The centre quadrangle of the building was destroyed by fire in February, 1873, and many valuable books and works of art lost, which can never be replaced. The damage done was estimated at thousands of pounds.

The Duke of Connaught (Prince Arthur) and the unfortunate Prince Imperial of France received their education at the Royal Military Academy as " Queen's Cadets," the Sovereign possessing the prerogative of nomination. A marble bust of Prince Arthur, in his cadet's uniform, stands in the Library. It was the work of his sister the Princess Louise. All candidates are eligible who can pass the requisite examination and medical inspection before entry.

In rear of the Royal Military Academy is a

MINERAL WELL,

the water of which is said to possess some valuable medicinal qualities; it is said that it never runs dry nor freezes. It is resorted to by invalids and others, and any one is welcome to a draught of its not unpalatable, though somewhat pungent, spring.

In speaking of the Buildings connected with the garrison, we may just mention, without enlarging upon them, the Herbert Hospital, at the top of Woolwich Common, completed about 1854; the permanent Camp of Huts on Woolwich Common, which have been filled with artillery and other troops since the Crimean War; the Cambridge Barracks in Frances Street, formerly the Royal Marine Barracks,* and now occupied nearly always by a regiment of infantry; the Red Barracks, lately the Royal Marine Infirmary, a new and really beautiful building; and the Military Church and other buildings in the Dockyard.

* These handsome Barracks stand on the site of Whitby's Brewery, purchase by the Government, in order to provide accommodation for the Royal Marinesd in 1807.

A TRIP TO WOOLWICH.

To Woolwich next, where noble ships have birth
  And war's dread engines slumbering lie in store,
Ready to desolate this peaceful earth,
  Plucking red laurels from a field of gore.

WOOLWICH is 8½ miles in a straight line from
Charing Cross, about 10 by rail, and 12 by the winding
river.   Like many other old waterside towns, it is not itself
attractive, and people who speak of its great garrison and wonderful workshops, its academies of military science, and its marvellous warlike productions, will tell you that Woolwich itself
has not much to recommend it to the eye.   But such persons

have probably gained their impressions from the prejudices of others, or have themselves paid but a flying visit to the place, and wandered about the not too-savory purlieus of the river-side wharves or railway stations, lost themselves for a few hours in an undirected ramble through the grimiest mazes of the Arsenal, and then returned home with the opinion that they have seen Woolwich, and that it is "a dirty place." Let the visitor, if he would do it justice, go to Woolwich on a fine day, and by water. He will find the Woolwich steamboats, which leave all the London piers two or three times every hour, clean, commodious, and comfortable, and as fast as the river regulations will permit. The journey will occupy about an hour, and ought to be a pleasant and instructive one, carrying the visitor as it does past the wealth of the world's commerce, flowing in and out of the great metropolis in mighty ships; past the "*Pool,*" with its forest of masts; past the great docks and ship-building yards; past *Greenwich,* with its world-renowned Observatory

GREENWICH HOSPITAL AND NAVAL COLLEGE.

on the heights of its beautiful park, and its magnificent pile of buildings down at the water's edge, once a Royal Palace, the birth-place of England's kings and queens—since then the home of England's worn out tars—and now the nation's Naval College and Museum, where its sea-cadets receive their instruction in navigation and the modern science of naval warfare; past *Blackwall,* its docks and shipping; and, at the other end of the broad reach of the river, *Woolwich* is before us. Its first appearance is decidedly in its favour. Backed by the beautiful slopes and ridges of Shooters' Hill and Plumstead Common and the lovely range of hills stretching away to Erith, the town, embosomed in woods and clothed in verdure, seems to rise up from the river to a considerable altitude, crowned most conspicuously by the handsome Red Barracks with its minaretted turrets, and by old-fashioned houses apparently heaped together in picturesque confusion. The ancient church of St. Mary stands out boldly in the midst of its well-filled churchyard, where even from the river we can see the great stone lion which surmounts the grave of " Tom Cribb," the famous British boxer, who lived and died at Woolwich, the peaceable proprietor of a baker's shop in High Street. Our forefathers wisely planted a row of elms before the church, which have now grown up into fine old trees and greatly improve its aspect by obscuring all but its not unsightly square tower—in which, by the way, there is a fine peal of bells. Before the steamboat reaches Woolwich, the passenger will note the telegraph factories of Messrs. Siemens Brothers, and the similar ones at *North Woolwich* and *Silvertown*; these several works have contributed to the comfort and enlightenment of mankind more, perhaps, than any others of their kind in the world, for from one or other of them have emanated most of the wondrous electric cables which now, sunk in the ocean, chain continents together in close communication and " put a girdle round about the world."

Near Charlton pier lies the " Warspite," an old warship which has been devoted to the use of the Royal Marine Society. On board this ship about three hundred poor boys, rescued from the streets of London, but unsullied by crime, are maintained and trained for sailors in the national and mercantile marine. Most of them readily find situations after about a year's preparation on board this ship; and the reports which the Society obtain respecting them afterwards are almost always good. It is a very excellent institution, and sends about 300 boys to sea every year. Passing Charlton Pier (sometimes called West Woolwich, for it is within the parish) the steamer will take our visitor past the ancient *Dockyard* of Woolwich, now no longer the great shipbuilding depot it has been for generations past, it having been closed as a dockyard in 1869. Part, a very small part, was then sold, but the bulk of the property was transferred from the Admiralty to the War Department, by whom its great factories,

WOOLWICH DOCKYARD, 1868.

and even some of its building slips, have been utilized as stores. The closing of the Dockyard, and the discharge of its many workmen, was a sad blow to Woolwich, and it was long before it recovered from the shock. On the opposite side of the river are the Pavilion Hotel and *North Woolwich Gardens*, the most popular of all the public gardens near London, and beyond are the Docks and the City of London Gas Works at Beckton; facing them the visitor will see the vast buildings and towering shafts of England's famous *Arsenal*. As it is to this, we presume, the visitor is bound, he will land at Roff's Pier and make the best of his way to the Arsenal gates, by way of Beresford Street.

There are other ways of reaching Woolwich than by the river, though on a fine day that is the most pleasant. Residents in the north or east of London will find it convenient to travel by rail to Blackwall or North Woolwich. Passengers can book from all stations in those parts to Woolwich Town, boat and rail inclusive, and the fares are very reasonable. Many, however, prefer the North Kent Line, which is the most direct route to London Bridge, Cannon Street, and Charing Cross, and connects Woolwich, through the District Railway, with the "far west." All these routes, unfortunately, land the visitor in some ancient back street; for the old part of Woolwich, like most old waterside

localities, is not inviting. Residents, however, are proud of its broad and beautiful Common, and the delightful scenery which surrounds them can hardly be equalled anywhere within the same distance of London, as the visitor may judge for himself if he will take the trouble to stroll up towards Shooters' Hill, either through Woolwich, Plumstead, or Charlton.

FRAGMENTS OF ROMAN FUNEREAL URNS

found (containing bones and ashes) in a deep excavation at the Dial
Square, Royal Arsenal, in 1856 ; the earliest archæological relics of
Woolwich known to exist ; probable date about A.D. 350.

HISTORY OF WOOLWICH.

A THOUSAND YEARS AGO !

WOOLWICH with a history of a Thousand Years ! Perhaps
not a written history ; but with the materials at our command, it seems no difficult task to picture what this Woolwich
was like, not merely a thousand years ago, but even in the more
remote periods of the past—periods of which the nation itself
possesses no written records. Its very name (that is its ancient
name) tells us what it was when the Saxons found it—when the
conquering hosts of Saxon Hengist drove back the half-savage
British battalions, and founded the Kingdom of Kent after the
battle of Creccanford or Crayford (A.D. 457). That name has
little changed to this day. It was originally " Wulewich," from
two Anglo-Saxon words, signifying, " the village on the bay," or
curve of the river ; and, although it is described in Domesday
Book (1086) as " Hulviz " (a dwelling on the creek), and has
been otherwise corrupted at various times, it has borne its

original appellation with tolerable accuracy until the present day, albeit time has rung some remarkable changes on the orthography, being at various eras written, Wlewich, Walwich, Wollewic, Woolwicke, Wolwych, Wolwich, Wulwiche, Woolwych, Woollwitche, and, finally, Woolwich. We have, indeed, evidence that even the pronunciation of its name, which has sometimes been attributed to what we vulgarly call Cockneyism is the same which it has borne for some three or four hundred years, for Sir Hugh Willoughby, writing in 1553, calls it "Woolich." But we have records far earlier than this, for in 964, King Edward endowed the Abbey of St. Peter at Ghent, "with certain land called Lewisham," in which Greenwich, Woolwich, and Mottingham are mentioned as being included as appurtenances; and the record in Domesday Book shows that in 1086, there was a very desirable freehold estate, as we should call it now, "consisting of 63 acres of land in Hulviz (Woolwich), in the Greenviz (Greenwich) Hundred, which William the

ANCIENT GATEWAY AT BARKING.

Falconer held of King Edward, the whole value of which is three pounds!" This estate, we learn, was leased to eleven "bordars," who paid forty-one pence. This is the only mention of Woolwich in the Domesday Book. Although, however, history is silent as to its remote antiquity, and its Anglo-Saxon title is the strongest evidence we have that Woolwich existed as a dwelling place a thousand years ago, we may be sure from its situation at the very foot of a beautiful hill, covered with woods, and close to a broad and noble river, that it must have been the favoured resort of our distant forefathers, even in the dark and uncivilized ages which preceded the advent of the Romans. At that time, however, the river at Woolwich was not merely the embanked channel we now find it, but a wide expanse of water, spreading over what is now marsh land on either side, from Abbey Wood on the south to Barking on the north, and it may be here remarked that in the earlier days of our Christianity, religious houses or monasteries existed at both these places, and a boat was dug up near the site of Lesness Abbey (Abbey Wood) not many years ago, in which, probably, the good old monks were accustomed to visit their brethren across the broad water at Barking. The days of old, when "wild in woods our savage fathers ran," saw

AN ANCIENT FOREST

on either side of the river, traces of which are still to be found on both banks, often running down the shelving shore a good way towards the middle of the channel. The Plumstead Marshes are full of bog-oak, trunks of willow, yew, and other trees, amongst which the workmen making the great main sewer turned up many an antler of the wild deer, and frequent traces of the boar and the ox; and it is not many years since an important work on the foreshore of the Royal Arsenal was delayed for some days by the men having to cut away the trunk of an oak tree into which they had driven. The clearest possible evidences of the ancient forest are to be seen at this day on the foreshore at Dagenham, near Barking Creek. At low water, the stumps of many old trees are uncovered, gradually changing their nature to that of coal-like peat. The best way to visit this spot is to take a boat from Woolwich or Crossness, which is nearly opposite. That the Romans occupied Woolwich there need be no question; its proximity to the great road ("Watling Street") which they cut from London over Shooters' Hill to Dover, which remains the great high road to this day, leads to the certain inference that they could not have overlooked such a desirable spot for residence, and, indeed, we have pretty certain evidences that a Roman hamlet did here once exist. Roman urns and fragments of Roman pottery have been dug up in the Royal Arsenal and the neighbourhood (notably a fine sepulchral vase now at the Royal Artillery Institution.)* Dr. Andrew Wynter says that a Roman cemetery occupied the site of the Royal Arsenal, and he moralises on the circumstance, saying that "Where the conquerors of the old world lay down to their last rest, we, the Romans of the present age, forge the arms which make us mas-

---

* See Illustration, Page 75.

ters of an empire beyond the dreams of the Imperial Cæsars."
Some of the urns in question contained bones, and the rest ashes.
They were certainly of Roman manufacture, and as cremation
ceased in England about the year 400, they must have been of
early date. There is little doubt that the town which the Romans
made stood for centuries where they established it, on the site to
which it was confined even to the boyhood of our oldest inhabitants, who can recollect Woolwich when it consisted only of the
few streets—then respectable, but now disreputable—which we
find huddled together by the river in the corner next the Arsenal
wall. To the abbots of

LESSNESS ABBEY

may probably be attributed the earliest importance of Woolwich,
for the fishermen who dwelt here by the river would have to
supply the recluses with much of their daily food. Lessness
Abbey, now crumbled to ruin, stood on the north side of Abbey
Wood, and the site, which is the property of Guy's Hospital,
and forms the farm buildings, garden, and orchard of Stapley's
farm, is about half a mile from Abbey Wood railway station.
The Abbey was founded in the year 1178, for monks of the
order of St. Augustine, by Richard de Lucy, when Henry II.
was king. De Lucy, who was first a soldier and then a friar,
was buried in the church; and in 1630, a hundred years after
the abbey had been suppressed and destroyed, some workmen,
digging among the rubbish, discovered what was doubtless his
monument, and beneath it a leaden coffin containing the remains
of a man. The relics are supposed to have been reburied near
the spot, but they have lately been searched for in vain. To the
abbots is given the credit (erroneously we believe) of having enclosed by river walls the marsh land on either side of the river,
thereby acquiring large tracts of rich and fruitful soil, quicken-
ing the flow of the river, and deepening its channel by the more
rapid scour. One authority on this point is William Lambarde,
who resided three hundred years ago at Westcombe, between
Charlton and Greenwich (there are West Combe and East Combe
at Charlton even now). He says that the Abbot of Lessness*
enclosed a portion of the marshes at Plumstead in 1279, and

---

* Lessness—From Anglo-Saxon *leas* (smaller or less) and *noesse* (a promontory
or hill.)

finished enclosing the whole by 1291; and upon this authority
it has been declared that in these twelve years the river wall
from Woolwich to Erith was built, and the tidal waters restrained.
The fact, no doubt, is, that the Abbot reclaimed some of the land
after one of the inundations which occasionally occurred, but the
great work of the river wall may be more feasibly assigned to
the Romans, who are said to have reclaimed all the marsh land
between London and Gravesend. Walker's Thames Report of
1841, says, "The probability is that these embankments are the
work of the Ancient Britons under Roman superintendence;
that they are the result of skill and bold enterprise, not unworthy
of any period, is certain." Sir Christopher Wren and others have
pronounced the work as of Roman origin; and Roman coins, originally "banked" by their owners hundreds of years ago, have
been dug out of the earthen wall quite recently. In 1236, the
Charlton marshes were inundated by a high tide, like that which
did so much damage in 1874; and we read that Henry III.,
appointed a commission "for the overseeing and repairing the
breaches, walls, ditches, &c., in divers places between Greenwich
and Woolwich." The Plumstead marshes appear to have
suffered a more disastrous deluge soon after Henry VIII.'s time,
the unsettled state of the Church and the convulsion of property
having probably led to the neglect of the river wall; a breach
then occurred at Erith, by which 2,000 acres were again deluged,
and were not again recovered until the time of King James I.,
when the wall was repaired and the water drained off by an
Italian engineer, at great labour and expense.

The old Abbey probably shared the fate which befel its sister
house at Barking, and most of the other establishments of the
kind, when Henry VIII. laid his hand upon them, and con-
fiscated them and their possessions without mercy or favour.

It is generally reported, in the histories and guide-books, that
there is not a stone of the old abbey standing, and these authorities, copying each other, assert that even the crumbling walls
which enclose the garden of the Abbey Farm are the remains of
a more recent building erected on the same spot; but any one
who visits the place under the guidance of the worthy and intelligent farmer who is now its proprietor, will be convinced that
these are errors, and will see some really ancient and interesting
ruins. There are especially two handsome archways left, which

are, undoubtedly, remains of the original abbey, though most of the walls have probably been rebuilt of the old materials. One of these arches led into the Chapel, the shape of which is still well defined, and the gardener's spade has often come upon its tesselated pavement three feet beneath the present surface. The walls may be traced far into the wood behind, and away to the right and left. There is a tradition that the old abbey was connected by a subterranean passage with Plumstead Church, and a few years ago a staircase was opened, which seemed to lead to a considerable depth, but it was filled in without being thoroughly explored. It is singular that a series of wells, or " chalk holes," as they are called, extend almost in a line between the ruins and the church at Plumstead. However, the subterranean passage may be open to doubt, but it would be absurd to disbelieve that in these ruins we stand within the very walls once inhabited by holy men, in

> Monastic beards and shaven crowns,
> And capes and hoods, and friars' gowns.

Relics of little intrinsic value, but of an interesting character, are often found in the soil, and we saw one day some of the farmer's men dig up a considerable length of old lead pipe, with which probably the good old monks got their water from the adjacent " Roman dock," as the deep hollow close by is called, from a legend handed down from generation to generation that it was here the Romans built their galleys. They were a wealthy corporation, these monks, having a broad estate, and if we find a little exaggeration in the songs which say—

> They sung and they laughed, and the rich wine quaffed,
> And they lived on the daintiest cheer—

we need have no hesitation in believing that they had a very delightful residence, and the means, at all events, of acting up to the maxim that—

> He who leads a good life is sure to live well.

PLUMSTEAD CHURCH,

which appears to have been an appurtenance of the Abbey, and has a history nearly 900 years old, has survived it 350 years, and has lately been restored; its ancient floor, which had been buried three feet in the dust of ages, and covered for two or three generations with a new flooring above all, has been again brought to light.

OLD WOOLWICH CHURCH.

stood sixty or eighty yards from the site of the present edifice, and we are unable to find the date of its erection, but it was probably very remote. In Ireland's History of Kent it is stated that the church, dedicated to St. Mary, was given by Henry I. (about the year 1100) to St. Andrew Gundulph, Bishop of Rochester, and the monks there, together with all the tithes, and that he afterwards by charter sustained them in possession. The church was confirmed to the Priory of Rochester in subsequent deeds, and it still remains in that diocese.* In 1464, William Preve, rector, built a chapel and bell tower, but in the course of years the church fell into decay; and at the beginning of the last century, £1,141 was collected by charitable contributions for its repair, Dr. Lindsay, Lord Primate of Ireland, and formerly rector of Woolwich, giving £380 towards it. The church, however, which appears to have been built of flints and chalk, was found too far gone for repair (the old vestry books say that it stood on a sandy hill—a dangerous site) and it was resolved to rebuild it entirely. So in 1726 the site of the present church was purchased, the old one having stood on the north side of the footpath which runs through the churchyard from High Street to Church Hill. An old pamphlet dated 1718, and entitled "Reasons for rebuilding Woolwich Church," states that "There is near 1,000 families belonging to the *Navy Dock Yard* and *Rope Yard*, 200 Families belonging to the *Ordnance Service*, and about 100 independant of either, which after the rate of 5 to each Family is 6,500, and the said old small church cannot (at most) contain above 600 People. . . And the Parish is very Populus and dayly increasing." Through this and other appeals, funds were obtained, and by an Act of George II., a grant of £3,000 was made for rebuilding this church as one of fifty ordered to be built in and near London, out of the coal dues collected in " the Pool." Thus was erected and completed in 1740, the building which we have learnt to call "*the old church*" too. Daniel Wiseman, Esq., who died in 1739, aged 65, left £1,000 for " finishing the new church at Woolwich," and there

---

* Recently, for a few years, it was in the diocese of London, but it has been restored to the see of Rochester.

is a monument to his memory on the south side of the chancel.
The total cost of the church was £6,500.*

WOOLWICH CHURCHYARD, (from Parson's Hill).

The old vestry books, which we have by the courtesy of the
Rector examined, supply some information on this and other
subjects connected with the church, which may be inserted here.
The oldest entry we find of a vestry meeting is dated 1669, and,
if we are to judge by the vestry books, public meetings were not
much in vogue, for the records are far between. The vestry
meetings, when they *were* held, always took place in the vestry
room after service on Sunday evenings, and it seems to have
been the custom of every one present to sign the book, for there
are numerous and curious collections of autographs. The first
churchwardens we read of are John Clothier and John Oliver,
who ruled peaceably in 1669, but we find no records worth
quoting until 1698, when some conscientious overseers entered
in full the payments they made out of the parish purse. Most
of the items are for relief distributed to wayfarers, and there are
very many entries like the following, which all occur in that
year :—

* The reconstruction of the Parish Church by the present generation is matter for
another edition of this history.

1698.—9 May—Relieved 3 men cast away, bound for Dover, 1s.

16 May—Relieved a minister who came from the North, bound to Canterbury, 1s.

This does not betoken much for the respectability of "the cloth" in those days. Here is another entry which would shock a modern sportsman; but foxes then were real "vermin," and vulpecide a virtue:—

16 May—Paid Robert Hopkins for a fox's head, 1s.

The following entries, be it remarked, related to the old churchyard, a small space now enclosed on the north side, nearest the Dockyard:—

1 July—Paid for cutting ye woods out of ye churchyard, 2s. 6d.

10 Nov.—Paid William Osborn for mending ye ways and carrying away ye rubbishe in ye churchyard; for stopping two sandholes; and for keeping ye boyes in order, 11s.

This seems cheap service if well performed, even to the extent of keeping the boys in order, but it must be borne in mind that a shilling of the present day does not in any way represent the value of a shilling 200 years ago. From the next en'ry it appears that King William III. disembarked at Woolwich after his visit to Holland in 1698:—

10 Dec.—Paid ye ringers when ye King landed, 7s. 6d. Also, paid ye ringers at another time when ye King returned from Holland, 7s. 6d.

There were "spongers" in the olden time if we may credit the following resolution, which appears under the 12th of May, 1716:—

Whereas, it hath been the constant practice of several inhabitants of this parish at the time of the perambulation of the bounds thereof, and also at the visitation, to resort to the place appointed by the churchwardens for those meetings, and there to intrude themselves, with no other intent or design than to *eat and drink*, and so put the parish to extraordinary charge: Ordered—That no inhabitant, saving the minister only, shall on those days have or partake of anything for Breakfast, Dinner, or otherwise, by the churchwardens' order, unless such person or persons who come with intent to go the said bounds, do first deposit or pay into the hands of the churchwardens eighteenpence towards the charges and expenses of the parish for that day.

Beating the boundaries, which had usually cost about £5, was required, about the same time, to be carried out for £3. It is no wonder that the ratepayers went in for retrenchment, for the

WOOLWICH AND ITS DOCKYARD IN 1790.

church-rate was not unfrequently "twelvepence" in the pound for the half-year, and the total amount this realised was less than £100, so that the burden was pretty heavy upon the few who had to bear it.

From one of the rates written in full, we learn that a large portion of what is now Plumstead was then assessed to Wool-wich, even as far down as Colefields—a name which is still preserved on the register of voters, though the fields have disappeared. They are represented, however, by the "Dover Castle," public-house and the locality thereabouts, and it is probable that the boundary of Woolwich then extended, as the boundary of the borough did (with a little variation) until lately, so as to include all the land between that point and the top of Sandy Hill. A pretty slice of territory to be lost by Woolwich through inattention—that which was then open country and little valued being now the site of a populous town. The overseers appear to have been always bickering with their neighbours at East Ham as to the boundaries at North Woolwich, but the insidious advances of their neighbours at Plumstead they heeded not. We may be conjecturing too much in expressing this belief, but it is confirmed by later entries, which include the assessment of "Burrage House" in Woolwich.

A resolution of December, 1723, forbids the cutting of furze on Woolwich Common; and in March, 1735, it was ordered "That the Cage, Watch-house, and Stocks be pulled down and rebuilt as before, on the same ground." These stood at the north end of Rope Yard Rails some twenty years ago, but in a ruinous state, the stocks disappearing some time before the stones.

The rebuilding of the church appears to have been the great work of that generation, and most of the vestry meetings relate to it. The piece of land on which it and the main part of the churchyard stands was bought of Mr. Richard Bowater, and one William Pook* was employed, under authority of a Royal Warrant, to collect subscriptions. These amounted to £2,328; Parliament, as before stated, voted £3,000, and Mr. Wiseman gave £1,000 of the remainder. A memorial in the vestry books, praying Parliament to sanction an annuity to Mr. Wiseman's mother and aunt, of 5 per cent. on this £1,000, is especially

---

* The Pooks were an old Woolwich family as recently as thirty years ago. Their descendants have now settled at Greenwich.

interesting, as it bears among its signatures that of Andrew Schalch, the master founder, and also that of Jacob Schalch, who, we believe, was his brother. In 1740, when the church was completed, it was resolved to sell the materials of the old church, and the present vestry was built with the proceeds. In the first half-year of 1741, the rates were " 12d." in the £ for the poor, and " 12d." for the decoration and " repair" of the new church.

The old parsonage house, which stood near the Thames, on the site of the shops standing to the west of the Consumers' Gas Works, was pulled down in 1809, and the present Rectory built in Rectory Place on the glebe land, which was then about twenty acres of pasture enclosed in a ring fence.* It is now covered with valuable houses.

The living was originally valued in the king's books at £7 12s. 6d. per annum. It is now worth about £800.

In a volume of sermons, published in 1796, by the Rev. G. A. Thomas, it is stated that the parish contained 10,000 inhabitants, and that his predecessor, who held the living thirty-nine years, had cleared only £100 a year, after a curate's salary and other expenses had been paid. Mr. Thomas adds that the occupiers of the " better half" of the parish at North Woolwich, had been in the habit of paying the rector only £20 a year, in lieu of tithes, for their land—400 acres—but that he demanded a more just arrangement, and was afterwards paid 5s. per acre. The present increased value of the living is, however, mainly due to the glebe-land being built upon. Mr. Morgan says that in his recollection, that is, in 1810, there was not a brick standing within the triangle represented by the top of Coleman Street, Mulgrave Place, and Powis Street, a space now occupied by a thousand houses.

A fine picture of Woolwich Dockyard, painted by Mr. Proctor in 1790 (a sketch of which we have introduced into the present edition of this work) shows Woolwich as it then was, a cluster of houses near the river, and the early Artillery Barracks standing out in the fields.

In the sacred soil of the old churchyard, where burials are no longer permitted, lie the ashes of many good and distinguished

---

* Hasted's History of Kent. Date, 1778.

men, but the attention of the passing visitor will be more especially arrested by such of the tombs as present some curious features. Amongst these there is one which records a diabolical murder, which much agitated Woolwich and created some interest throughout the country more than fifty years ago. The inscription on the stone, nearly obliterated, says :—

"Underneath this ground is interred all that remains of Thomas Parker, Esq , of Woolwich, where he lived for twenty-four years, an unblemished man. He was barbarously murdered and his house set on fire, March 3rd, 1820, aged 78. Thirty yards north of this stone lieth Sarah Brown, his house-keeper and faithful servant, slain by the hand of the same ruffian."

The grave of Tom Cribb, the pugilist, is, perhaps, the most conspicuous in the churchyard, being surmounted with the stone figure of a lion, which has one of its paws placed upon a funeral urn. The inscription is "Thomas Cribb, born July 8th, 1781; died May 11th, 1848. Respect the ashes of the dead." It is recorded to the especial honour of Tom Cribb that, amid the proverbial corruption of that *noble* institution the British prize-ring, "he never sold a fight."

Tom Griffiths, another prize-fighter, who was killed in a pugilistic contest on the 23rd of July, 1850, in the 27th year of his age, is buried close to Cribb.

Epitaphs were greatly in vogue at one time, and the churchyard presents two remarkable instances. These moral tombstones are both placed close beside the public footpath, so that the passer-by may read, mark, and learn therefrom. Poor Charlotte Rees, aged 17, was accidently killed on the 4th of March, 1839, through the discharge of a gun from a neighbour's premises. It was in Tappy's Place, Powis Street, and she was sitting in one of the wooden cottages, which then abounded, when a bullet came through the thin wall and by an unhappy mischance, struck her in the head. One side of the gravestone is filled with a long sermon on the uncertainty of life, and the epitaph is on the other. The fourth verse tells us the sad story in a few words :—

No one was present when the fatal ball
Entered, by accident, the cottage wall ;
But in a moment she who lays below
Sunk prostrate under death's relentless blow.

On the opposite side of the footpath we may see through the railings the grave in which were buried " the five boys who were drowned on the ice in Bowater pond on Sunday, the 6th of February, 1831," and the stone relates that " the jurors who were present at the coroner's inquest caused this memorial to be erected as a public contribution to commemorate the mournful event, but more especially to impress upon the young the necessity and importance of remembering their Creator in the days of their youth, and to excite them to avoid the sin and danger of violating the Sabbath day."   Of the verses on the other side, one is sufficient :—

> That holy morn in blooming health they rose,
> But on their bier were laid before its close ;
> For scorning God's command and friends' advice,
> They sank and drowned beneath the faithless ice.

Maudsley, the eminent engineer, who was born in Salutation Alley, Woolwich, and began life as a powder-boy in the Royal Arsenal, lies buried on the north side of the churchyard.   The grave of Andrew Schalch is near the same spot.

Lovelace, the cavalier poet (1618), was born at Woolwich, at the house of Sir William Lovelace, his father.   A man of another sort, Joseph Grimaldi, the prince of stage clowns, lived and died at Woolwich.

When Woolwich first assumed the character of a

NAVAL STATION,

is a little uncertain.   Bishop Gibson. pronounces it the oldest Royal Dockyard in the kingdom, and it has been positively asserted, over and over again, that the first great man-of-war England possessed, the " Great Harry," was built at Woolwich ; but it has also been confidently averred that the credit of producing the famous ship is due to Erith, while others declare with equal certainty that the honour belongs to Purfleet.   The "Great Harry" was built in 1512, and we infer that if the Dockyard had been at that time established, it was not very extensive, for we find that in the reign of Henry VIII., the monarch bought of Sir Edward Boughton, then proprietor of the manor of Southall or Woolwich, two parcels of land there called Boughton's Docks, and two other parcels called Sand Hill and Our Lady Hill.   The docks were necessarily at the waterside.   We have a Sandy Hill to the present day, but the two hills mentioned are probably those through which the railway tunnels are cut, near the Dockyard. However, it appears pretty evident that in the reign of Henry VII. Woolwich Dockyard was in existence, and, although it has now been disestablished (350 years after), naval authorities still concur in saying that the king, who has been called the "father of the navy," could not have selected a more judicious site for the birthplace of his children. In his reign several small ships appear to have been built at Woolwich, but the first vessel worthy of notice, of which we have any authentic record, was launched here in the reign of his successor, Henry VIII. Having lost his finest ship, the "Regent," during an engagement with the French off Brest, "bluff King Harry" is said to have gone into a towering passion, and ordered the construction of a man-of-war which should astonish the world. This was the "Harry Grace de Dieu," a vessel which in that era must have been regarded, and justly so, as a magnificent production. She was of 1,000 tons burden, and carried 122 guns, but they were mostly of small calibre, all but 13 being less than 9-pounders.

Queen Elizabeth visited Woolwich Dockyard on the 3rd of May, 1559, to be present at the launching of a large ship christened after Her Majesty, the "Elizabeth." In 1637, a wonderful ship, the "Royal Sovereign," was built. Corresponding with the date, she had a burden of 1637 tons, and was 128 feet long by 48 feet beam. She was pierced for 116 guns, and even in the present day would be regarded as a fine ship. She was elaborately carved and gilt, after the fashion of the time, and the Dutch, amongst whom she played serious havoc, called her the "Golden Devil."

Through the long roll of mighty ships which have been built at Woolwich, we shall, however, not attempt to go; but we may say that many of the old wooden walls which have sailed o'er the sea to attest Britannia's power, but are fast disappearing before the ironclad "monsters of the deep," were launched here, and Woolwich is indelibly associated with all the grand victories which, from the days of Drake to the days of Nelson, have won for this little isle her proud position among the nations of the earth. The Dockyard was considerably enlarged early in the present century, by taking in a large tract of land at the

G

western end, where the steam-engine factory was afterwards built, and large basins constructed. As a ship-building yard it was finally closed in 1869, in accordance with the recommendation of a Parliamentary Committee, which advised the abolition of the yards at Deptford, Woolwich, and a few other places, and the enlargement of the remaining establishments. The motive seems to have been ecomony, but the act led to much suffering among the families of the discharged artizans, and for several years the whole town, especially the locality near the Dockyard, suffered deep adversity.

Woolwich made considerable strides in the development of its warlike character during the reign of George II., full of wars as it was with Spain, France, and the Pretender. It was during this busy time that a mutiny broke out among

THE WOOLWICH ROPE MAKERS.

There were about 400 of these employed in the Rope-walk, the site of which (for it has long disappeared) is indicated by Rope Yard Rails. It is said that these men, with a desire to enhance the value of their labour, refused to take apprentices, and that the King to puuish them, had eight of them impressed for sailors. This the others resented by going in a body and volunteering for the Navy, and as the supply of cables for the ships was thus stopped, the Government was glad to send them all back, and the men, at least for a time, gained the victory. The rope-walk was 400 yards in length.

Woolwich, which has always been the head-quarters of

THE ROYAL ARTILLERY,

appears also to have been its birthplace. The regiment was formed during the reign of George I., about 150 years ago. Previous to that period, two or more guns were attached to each battalion of infantry. For a long time Artillery was only employed in siege operations, and, even after the introduction of field guns, it was many years before the force was in anything like an efficient state.

Contemporary with the advance which was being made with the Artillery force about the beginning of the eighteenth century, the science of gun-making made rapid strides at

THE ROYAL ARSENAL,

of which we give a full history in another part of this book. The Royal Artillery Barracks was at that time in the Warren or Arsenal, and it is stated in the *Gentleman's Magazine* for October, 1745, that 200 gunners, bombardiers, and matrosses started from Woolwich with a large train of Artillery for the defence of the West of England against the French. In the same month another artillery train left Woolwich, consisting of fifteen 3-pounder guns, eleven waggons of military stores, two smiths' forges, and nine carriages loaded with gunpowder and ball, to defend the north of England from the advance of "Prince Charlie." This force was accompanied by a hundred men, of whom part were mattrosses—half soldiers and half labourers—which was decidedly not overmanning the guns, though they were only 3-pounders. Indeed, the force at this date was so inefficient, that we read of a battery of artillery in one action being lost through the combined badness of the horses and the roads. The battery of eight guns had to be abandoned, except one which was dragged away by the "Grenadiers," and horses and all were lost.

A REVEL IN THE "GOOD OLD DAYS."

There appears in the *St. James's Chronicle*, of 1764, an entertaining description of what we should now call a " fete," given in honour of the Marquis of Granby, who was at that time Master of the Ordnance, a position of great authority, which he appears to have occupied with much ability and popularity. One of the oldest public houses in Woolwich still bears his name as a sign, and if we may credit the posthumous records of the Pickwick Club, the fame of the Marquis gained him a similar honour at Dorking. The festival was on the Marquis of Granby's birthday, and the account we quote says that in the evening " there was a magnificent firework played off on the green in Woolwich Warren, and many pieces which had never before been exhibited.　A transparency was also shown, bearing the inscription, 'Long live Granby.'　During the time the piece was burning, the numerous spectators made great acclamation, and every heart was filled with joy.　After the fireworks, Colonel Williamson and the officers of the Royal Artillery, accompanied by many gentlemen of distinction, repaired to the Ship Tavern, where an elegant entertainment was provided for their reception."　There has been many an elegant entertainment at the Ship since it first stood sentinel at the Dockyard Gates, but we cannot boast of many occasions in these degenerate days when " every heart is filled with joy."

A ROYAL ARTILLERY MUTINY

took place at the barracks of the Royal Artillery in 1797, and seems to have been a serious affair, but we must remember that the discipline of the army on the one hand, and the condition of the soldier on the other, were very different to what we now find them.　The artillerymen complained of their food, which was bad in quality and insufficient, and, in order to draw attention to their grievances—as writing to the papers was not then in the fashion—they turned their officers out of barracks, and proclaimed themselves in a state of siege.　The terms of surrender were notified to the outer world by boards which were hung out demanding " more pay and less drill," but it is to the credit of the men that, all the while this extraordinary state of things lasted, they performed the garrison duties as strictly as though they had been under the closest surveillance.　The Government sent down commissioners to reason with the mutineers, promising to enquire into and remedy their hardships, and so the affair ended satisfactorily.　But such a demonstration would not answer now-a-days.

THE ROYAL ARTILLERY BARRACKS,

facing Woolwich Common, was building about the time of the mutiny before mentioned, part of the old Ordnance Hospital (now the Army Service Corps Barracks) having been built just before, and the Royal Military Academy shortly afterwards.　Descriptions of these buildings will be found in their proper places.

In the beginning of the present century, the local legislature sold its rights over

WOOLWICH COMMON

to the Board of Ordnance for the sum of £3,000, which was afterwards spent in a vain attempt to remove the parish market from High Street to a new market place, on which the Town Hall,* Parish-yard, and Police Station now stand. The purchase-money paid for the Common seems small, but more than half the ground is in the parish of Charlton, and that portion had to be purchased of Sir Thomas M. Wilson, the lord of the manor.

The beautiful grounds of the Royal Military Repository, the greater part of the Barrack Field, and the site of the Royal Artillery Barracks and Hospital, were purchased of Mr. Bowater.† He was one of the wealthiest men of the neighbourhood, and resided in a mansion near the site of the Cambridge (late Royal Marine Barracks).

THE GREAT WAR

with the First Napoleon gave an impetus to Woolwich, the force of which has never been exhausted. All the departments of the Royal Arsenal were largely augmented to meet the demand for war material, and the importance of field artillery as a weapon of war became for the first time established to such an extent that the Royal Regiment was recast on a much extended scale, and the manufacturing departments were filled with men and machinery to produce the indispensable guns. Even when the war terminated at the fall of Napoleon, in 1815, it was felt that the fortune of Woolwich was made, and though there were, of course, some reductions in the Arsenal when the strife ceased, it was clear that the altered circumstances which had taken place in the national works must, to a certain extent, remain permanent. The town, which at that time was little more than the High Street, and a few taverns gathered about the gates of the Arsenal and Dockyard, began to spread, labour was plentiful, wages high, and

---

* The first Town Hall was converted into the present Police Court, and a new hall built adjacent. See "Chronology."

† See Old Map, Page 101.

trade abundant.   At the peace rejoicings in 1814, when it was
fondly hoped that the scourge of Europe, Napoleon Buonaparte,
was securely held prisoner at Elba, Woolwich was still busy
making fireworks for the displays in the London Parks, and the
festival was not without its sacrifices, for several people were
killed either by premature explosions at the Royal Laboratory, or
the crushes in the parks.   In the same year the Emperor Alexander of Russia, the King of Prussia, Prince Blucher, and many
distinguished generals who were in England to share the rejoicings at the downfall of their common foe, came to Woolwich with
George the Third, visited the Arsenal, and witnessed a review on
the Common.   But 1815 was not a month old, when the escape
of Napoleon from Elba renewed the sanguinary conflict, and
Woolwich was the scene of continued activity.   When Napoleon
was finally and tightly chained to the rock at St. Helena, a few
months later, peace came to the land, and, the War with the
United States being settled about the same time, Woolwich,
though it never returned to its former self, experienced a relapse,
and fell into comparative stagnation.   The town continued to
progress notwithstanding, and a large and flourishing community
was established, in whose days we find the record of many names
familiar to this day and generation.   The first

GAS WORKS

were erected in Woolwich about 1820.   A tradesman in Hare
Street had for some time previously exhibited the new illuminating
power in his shop windows, but it was not till 20 years after that
gas superseded oil in the public lamps.   Indeed, the old oil lamp
did not altogether disappear from the streets until 1849, when
two important companies had long been at work supplying the
public with the now indispensable light.

THE CHURCHES AND CHAPELS,

leaving the old church out of the question, began to have a history only at the extremity of the last century.   In 1796 there
were (according to the enumerations made by Lysons*) six meet-

---

* Environs of London (Lysons) 1796.

ing houses in Woolwich, one belonging to the Presbyterians, two to the Anabaptists, two to the disciples of Mr. Whitfield, and one to those of Mr. Wesley. The earliest of these was at the bottom of Meeting House Lane, now an obscure alley running out of the dingiest part of High Street. Of the chapels which still exist, the first appears to have been that called "Enon," which was established in High Street by the Baptists; but other denominations followed as the town grew populous. The first Methodist Chapel stood on the ground now occupied by the Steam Flour Mills in New Road. The present Wesleyan Chapel at the top of William Street was built in 1816, and the Roman Catholics then took the old Wesleyan Chapel, and consecrated it as a church, in which they worshipped until their present church of St. Peter was built in 1843. Public buildings for meetings, concerts, and such like occasions being scarce at Woolwich fifty years ago, the old Catholic chapel was frequently used for those purposes. It was a barn-like structure, surmounted by a large cross. Before they had this chapel, good Catholics used to attend mass at Greenwich. "Woolwich Chapel," which has successively been the Ordnance Chapel and the Royal Arsenal Church, was built in a gravel pit at the entrance of Plumstead Road, by Dr. Percy, a year or two before 1800, and the form of worship there adopted was originally Independent or Congregational. The building, which is near to the Arsenal Gates, was sold by its founder to the Board of Ordnance, and was devoted to the use of the military of the garrison. It afterwards came to be used exclusively by the corps of Sappers and Miners, and has since, after many vicissitudes, been relegated to the officials and workmen of the Royal Arsenal. Salem Chapel, in Powis Street, now converted into a London School Board School, was established in 1798, by the Rev. Joseph Wilcox Percy, brother to the before-mentioned Doctor. When he died in 1820,* he

---

* In 1820 there was an educational movement in the town. At this time only two small schools for the poor were in existence in Woolwich—one in Rope Yard Rails, which was built and endowed in 1754 by Mrs. Ann Withers, who presented the organ to St. Mary's Church, and a day-school in connection with Enon Chapel. Now, the National Society established a school in the old Masonic Hall, Powis Street, and the British and Foreign School Society established another just opposite, in what had been the Woolwich Theatre. The Bickerdikes also established a respectable commercial school in Martin's Lane (now Burrage Road). The early labourers in these schools were Messrs. Miskin, Cheshire, Lever, and Buchanan. Mr. Cohen also rendered valuable assistance as a teacher.—(B. WELLS.)

was buried beneath the pulpit of his chapel. Salem Chapel continued to flourish until about the year 1850, when a vigorous offshoot, which ultimately became the prosperous Congregational Church in Rectory Place, seemed to withdraw the sap from the parent trunk, and it dwindled to its fall.

Trinity Church, in Beresford Street, was built on part of the old Rope Walk, about the year 1834, and was at first a proprietary church, but subsequently became a chapel of ease, in connection with the parish church of St. Mary.* St. John's, now in a district of its own, was consecrated early in 1847, and St. Thomas's, for many years an ecclesiastical district, separate from the rest of the parish, was formed a few years after, and its church built in Maryon Road. The beautiful church in the Dockyard was erected by the Government somewhat earlier, for the accommodation of the Royal Marines and the Dockyard people; the still grander "cathedral" church of St. George, as the garrison church is called, being of recent date, having been built in substitution of the church which for many years formed part of the Artillery Barracks—the church in which, by the way, Sims Reeves, the great English tenor, sang his first notes.†

The Presbyterians built their church in New Road about the same time as the Catholics built theirs, and there stood a public-house, the "Gun," between them. The Government, which contributes to the annual expenses of both these churches, on account of the soldiers who attend them, bought the public-house about 1854, and both the Presbyterians and the Catholics have now added to their churches excellent schools. The "North Britons" formed such a small colony in Woolwich fifty years ago, that a small building at the corner of Powis Street, in Green's End (surrounded by trees), sufficed for them all. They have now two fine churches, the second of which, called St. Andrew's, has been built in Anglesea Road within the last few years.

FIFTY YEARS AGO!

Only fifty years ago there was no communication between Woolwich and London except the passage-boats, which left daily

---

* The Rope Ground was abolished in 1833, and Beresford Street was built on the ground that it had occupied.

† Sims Reeves was born at Woolwich, his father being a musician in the Royal Artillery Band.

with the tide, and one old-fashioned and uncomfortable coach, which started from the " Crown and Anchor" (a little one-storey house), in High Street, every morning for Gracechurch Street, and returned every evening.   The fare by this "diligence" was five shillings each way, and a journey to London was in those days a matter of some consequence, not only for the time and money it cost, but for the dangers of the road ; which, beside being rough to travel, was frequented by highwaymen and foot-pads.   The passage-boats were rowed by the watermen all the way to and from London, and occupied two or three hours each journey on a fair tide.   As they always took advantage of the tide, passengers had often to get up at three o'clock in the morning to " catch the boat."   Generally, three wherries were sufficient for all the traffic, which makes the passenger list number about a score per diem.   Reckoning the same number for the coach, we have forty travellers from Woolwich to London daily. There are now at least four thousand.

About 1830 omnibuses began to run to and from London, and in 1834 the Woolwich Steam Packet Company was established, the first boat which ran from " Strother's Wharf," in High Street, being the " Sylph."   There are now upwards of thirty fine vessels, well known upon the Thames, but we can well understand and appreciate the great advance it was in those days to have such a ready and rapid communication opened, which caused the local poet to break out in a pæan of congratulation in the following strain :—

> To bear you o'er the waves in state,
>   Though wind and tide contrary,
>   A " Sylph" and three attendants wait—
>   A " Naiad," " Nymph," and "Fairy."

The North Kent Line was not opened till 1849, but the Eastern Counties ran a branch to North Woolwich shortly before.

Fifty years ago a group of low roofed cottages stood in Beresford Square, as it was called in honour of the Marquis of Beresford.   Green's End was another group of old houses, so called because they were at the extremity of the Sapper's Green, a sort of open common which stood where Wellington Street has since been cut and built.   There were a few cottages on the right hand side going up the hill, but the only public way was a narrow footpath between hedges and across stiles, which led from Green's End to Charlton. This footpath still exists, and though far different in appearance, it bears its old and once appropriate name—Love Lane. The high road to Charlton and London was Mill Lane, following a devious course, but there was, as at present, an alternative route by the Lower Road.

Fifty years ago the manners and customs were very different to those of the present day, and this will especially strike a Government employé in the fact that fifty years ago an hour a day was allowed in all the Royal Arsenal for "watering-time." For half-an-hour every morning, and half-an-hour every afternoon, work was suspended, and barrels of beer were brought in from the public-houses to keep up the spirits and energies of the workmen. This custom was abolished in 1829, and the abolition caused some heart-burning at first, but every one will admit now that the step was a judicious one.

Fifty years ago Woolwich Dockyard was at the height of its glory, and the Government bought a large piece of ground containing many houses, and threw it into the yard, in order to build the steam-engine factory and the basins.

A HUNDRED YEARS AGO.

Let us try to describe to the Woolwich resident of to-day what Woolwich was like a hundred years ago. This is rendered simple by a study of two or three old maps or plans still in existence. One is a sketch-plan, made in 1773, for the erection of the Royal Artillery Barracks, and the other (which we publish at page 101) is a part of the survey of Kent, 1778. They agree tolerably, and we find, by reference to them, that Woolwich, so far as houses made the town, consisted of High Street, and what we now call Cannon Row, and the lanes down to the waterside, with a few rows of dwellings to the western end of the parish by the "King's Yard." Love Lane footpath was the only direct way to Charlton,* and the road to Woolwich Common from the Warren was called Cholick Lane. The mill which stood a few

---

* An old newspaper paragraph under date of 1806, speaks of the "new road just opened from the west part of the Barracks to Charlton." From Green's End to the Farm House which then stood at the corner of Frances Street, there was only a foot-path for many years after. This footpath (Love Lane) is not marked in the Survey of 1778.

years ago on the site of the Engineer Offices in Mill Lane, existed even then; and nearly opposite it a road crossed the Common (where now is the Barrack Field) and a tavern called "The
Jolly Shipwrights" stood at the corner, just where we now see
the White Gate. The present road across the Common was
made years afterwards farther to the south of the old road; and
the road from the town to Shooters' Hill appears to have been
an ill-defined way, straggling past a few houses which had been
built on the edge of the Common. Another road, a continuation
of Frances Street, extended from near the "Jolly Shipwrights"
to the Dockyard Gates,* and there was a road now extinct, or
nearly so, from the cross roads at Shooters' Hill (near the present police station), over the Common,† and through Hanging
Wood to the Lower Road, emerging between the hills near Sand
Street, where the end of the ancient way and some of the old
houses still exist. Some remains of it are also found where it
crossed Little Heath, and the road at Woodland Terrace, where
it suddenly gets wider, is, no doubt, part of the same way.
Thence it wound in a devious course under the hills past Mount
Place, and out nearly opposite the "Lord Howick," and so on
to the ferry stairs, which the old advertisements might have announced as the "nearest landing place for Shooters' Hill."
There was also a footpath direct from Woolwich Church to
Cholick Lane and Plumstead, following the course now taken
by Rectory Place, and it does not need a very old memory to
recollect part of this remaining, and passing through a stile opposite the end of Mulgrave Place. It was in exchange for this
old thoroughfare that the Board of Ordnance gave the parish
St. John's Passage and the right of way to the White Gate.

At the beginning of the present century the Royal Marine
Barracks stood in the Dockyard, and the exercising ground was
the small open space in front of the Black Eagle. The bricked

---

* The sign of "The Jolly Shipwrights" was afterwards, when the old inn
was abolished, transferred to a tavern near the Dockyard Gates, now called the
"Globe."

† This road, which remained until a few years since from Shooters' Hill to
the corner of Cemetery Lane, was closed by the Government, and the present circular road to the Royal Military Academy was substituted. It was at the time
declared that the road was of modern origin, and no "right of way." The road
was, in fact, one of the oldest in the locality, being the most direct route from
the ferry and landing place at Charlton, to Shooter's Hill and the country beyond

up doorways are still discernible in the Dockyard wall. At the same period the Militia had their head-quarters in the Hall ("Alexandra") in Powis Street, and their guard-room in Union "Gardens."

A hundred years ago and less, Hanging Wood extended to the Common, and covered the whole slope of the Little Heath hill, except, perhaps, the "little heath" or roadside green which gave its name to the spot, for the Charlton road even is a modern creation, and that for many years came no nearer the heart of Woolwich than the corner of the Barracks at Frances Street. Wood Street and the "Woodman" were formerly part of the wood; and the shady glades of the Royal Military Repository in the valley where the wood ended, still show how lovely a valley it was. The ground, as we have said already, was the property of Mr. Bowater, whose residence was well called "Mount Pleasant." The "New Cross" in the map we cannot explain, unless it refers to the new cross, or road cut across Mr. Bowater's land to Woolwich church.

A study of this old map will be very interesting to any one acquainted with the locality.

From some curious old newspapers we cull some "elegant" extracts :—

In 1730, we read a long and circumstantial account of a street row. A prize-fight was being held at the "Tower," alehouse, (probably in Warren Lane, behind Rupert's Tower) and an "officer of the Dockyard had words concerning the fighting with one of the Train of Artillery, who gave him several blows with his fist. The other said he would fight him with swords, or any one of the Train; upon which several of the Matrosses knocked him down, and, running out of the door with their swords drawn, swore they would kill all the Townsmen they came near. All this created much indignation and commotion, the drummers beat to arms, and the Artillery Company marched up from the Warren in a warlike manner. The Riot Act was read, and orders given to fire on the people, but not obeyed. Four files of musketeers, however, were ordered to march round the town and to make everybody go indoors, and if they refused, to knock them down." This instruction they obeyed so implicitly that the "parish constable and his watch ordered them to their bar-

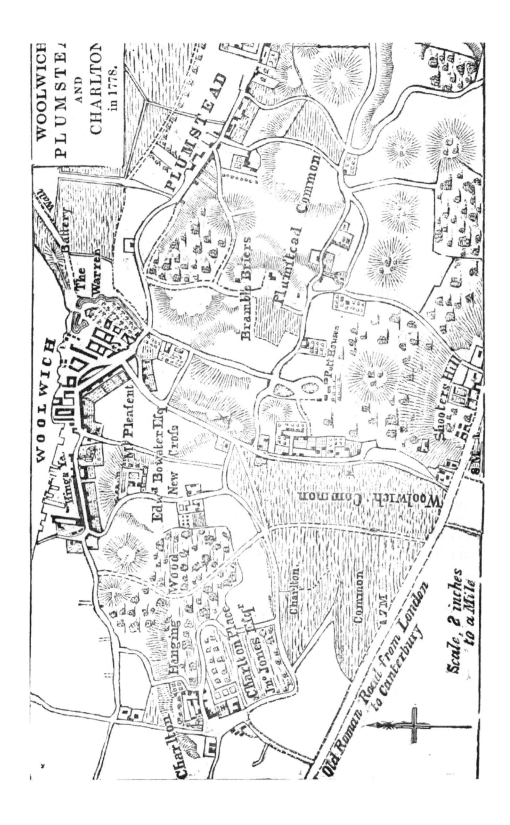

WOOLWICH
PLUMSTEAD
AND
CHARLTON
in 1778.

WOOLWICH

PLUMSTEAD

The Warren

Well

Battery

Bramble Briers

Plumstead Common

Plumstead

Putt Houses

Shooters Hill

PARK

Woolwich Common

Common

8M

King's Yard

Mr Pleasant

Edwd Bowater Esqr

New Cross

Hanging Wood

Charlton Place

Jno Jones Esqr

Charlton.

Charlton

1/2M

Old Roman Road from London to Canterbury

Scale, 2 inches to a Mile

racks, which they not only refused, but stabbed one of the watch, Mr. Thomas Smith, in the left breast."*

We read of an old-fashioned "strike" under date of May, 1757:—" Yesterday afternoon a detachment of 400 men belonging to the Foot Guards marched to Woolwich to quell the riotous workmen in that Dockyard. It has been the custom of these men to take away the chips they make as often as they go to their meals, but this has been grossly abused, and a stop has been put to the practice, which has been the cause of much grumbling and disaffection, and 'tis feared must end in some mischief."

The men, however, seem eventually to have got the better of the dispute, as the following " par" shows :—March 9th, 1770. " Wednesday last being the birthday of the Earl of Egmont, the morning was ushered in at Woolwich by the ringing of bells; flags and colours were displayed, and every possible demonstration of joy was shown on the occasion by the shipwrights, &c. The reason is that a few years since an attempt was made to debar the shipwrights from taking away their daily load of chips, but which his lordship got secured to them, as also a salary of £20 per annum for such as might become incapable; whereas they formerly were dismissed as soon as they became incapable, and left to the care of the parish."

The following are miscellaneous :—

1769.   " Yesterday morning was married at Woolwich, George Bond, Esquire, to Miss Norris, of Woolwich, an agreeable young Lady with a genteel Fortune."

1770.   " Last Saturday, Aug. 25th, their Majesties honoured the Regiment of Artillery with their presence in the Warren, at Woolwich. . . . . . They proceeded to the waterside, where several shots were fired from an iron gun by means of a lock being fixed to the vent. A sea-service 13-in. mortar was next fired three or four times, entirely filled with pound shot, which had a very good effect."

---

* Mr. Barnett, late parish surveyor of Woolwich, has in his possession a curious relic of the old town, being a pewter pint pot which was found in excellent preservation on the site of the old Cage in High Street, in excavating for the foundations of St. Saviour's Church, 1873. It is inscribed " Mary Hogg, at ye Bull Head, in Woolwich, 1726." Tradition says that a tavern called the Bull's Head, formerly stood near Market Hill, but all traces of it are lost. Two other pint pots were found a few years since bricked up in a wall in the Royal Arsenal, where some bygone joker had placed them a hundred years before.

1770. " Taken away by violence from her friends at Woolwich, by breaking open the locks of her chamber and parlour doors, and forcing her out of the window, Mary Baker: she is not 15 years old, has a speck in each eye, dressed in an old linen bedgown, with no stays on, a light-coloured quilted petticoat, and a red cloak, under the pretence of an arrest for debt, by John Davis. And supposed to be concealed by John Spencer, about 18 years old, son-in-law of the said John Davis. This is to caution all persons not to secrete or harbour the said Mary Baker, all clergymen are desired not to marry them, and all innkeepers and stable-keepers are not to furnish such persons with post-chaises or carriages. Whoever will bring the young Lady unmarried to Cuthbert Andrews, at his Majesty's Rope Yard, at Woolwich, will receive 20 guineas reward."

1776. " On Saturday there was another proof of cannon on Woolwich Common, before Lord Townsend . . . . after which, his Lordship examined all the young cadets at Woolwich, in order to see who were fit to be commissioned. They all dined afterwards at the New Tavern, on Woolwich Common."

1777. (Advertisement.) " Three genteel brick houses for sale at Charlton, in Kent, a village much esteemed for its healthful situation, rural walks, and pleasant ride. Four stage coaches goe through it every day, and return in the evening."*

1778. " His Majesty has ordered the Company of Cadets at Woolwich, to be augmented from 48 to 100."†

1779. (Advertisement.) " Whereas, his Majesty has been graciously pleased to give all gallant young men an opportunity of signalizing themselves, by augmenting his Royal Regiment of Artillery. This is to give notice to all spirited young fellows of good character, 5 feet 6⅓ inches high, that upon applying to the adjutant at Woolwich, they will be received into present pay, and shall all receive new cloathes, arms, and accoutrements proper for a gentleman of Royal Artillery."

---

* The Dover Road passes through Charlton.

† The Marquis of Granby, who was Master General of the Ordnance in 1764 reorganized the Academy, and placed it on a better footing. He increased the number of the cadets, obtained more able professors, increased the pay of each cadet from 1s. 4d. to 2s. 6d. per diem, and placed a bar on easy admission by instituting a qualifying examination. The dress of a gentleman cadet at this period was knee breeches, dark blue coatee, a cocked hat, somewhat similar to that worn by a Greenwich pensioner, and pig-tail.—(B. WELLS.)

1780, June 13th.—" On Wednesday, expresses arrived at Woolwich from the Secretary of State, that a large mob were assembling, determined to march to that place in order to set fire to the laboratory, store-houses, &c., and release the convicts; upon which the General beat to arms, and posted both officers and men to upwards of 30 guns, loaded with case-shot. . . . The matches were always alight, and everything ready to fire. . . . There never was a set of officers more active and vigilant than those of the Artillery on this occasion."

1807. " Mr. Fell, jun., of Plumstead, and Capt. Thomas, of the Marines, having agreed to fight a duel, Mr. Fell was arrested, and taken before the magistrates sitting at the ' Barrack Tavern,' Woolwich Common, and admitted to bail to keep the peace. The officers also, with considerable difficulty, found Capt. Thomas, who was liberated on giving similar security."

LOCAL GOVERNMENT, &C.

Woolwich has a Local Board of Health, constituted under the provisions of the Public Health Act, 1848, and the Local Government Acts of subsequent years. Previous to its formation, the town was governed by a Board of Commissioners, who had a variety of special powers conferred upon them by special Acts of Parliament. There was a local act of 1807, which authorized the Commissioners to seize, not only illegal weights and measures, but all loaves of bread which were short in weight, and give them to the poor.

The drainage and paving of the town have been carried out by the Local Board, the former having been executed in the years 1853-4, for the sum of £21,500, raised on loan for thirty years, which the inhabitants have since been paying. In addition to the cost of the main drains, the connections of the houses, or " private improvement " works, cost about £10,000 and there was also a private improvement loan for that purpose, now nearly extinguished.

When an order came from the Government to close the church-yard in 1855, the parish purchased the ground upon which its beautiful cemetery stands, between Plumstead Common and East Wickham. The amount borrowed for buying and laying out the ground was £6,200, and it has since been repaid.

Woolwich forms part, for Poor Law purposes, of the Woolwich Union, which comprises Woolwich, Plumstead, Charlton, and Kidbrook.

AREA, POPULATION, &c.

Woolwich contains 1,126 acres of land, and is divided in two by the river Thames, about equal portions of the parish being on either side. Owing to this singular situation, with the traffic to and from all parts of the globe passing between its two divisions, it is quaintly said that "more wealth passes through Woolwich than through any other town in the world." The river at Woolwich is 2,000 feet wide at high water. Its depth in the middle of the channel is 40 feet at high tide, and 20 feet at low water.

In fifty years Woolwich has more than doubled itself, both in houses and in population, as will be seen from the following quotations from the censuses of 1821 and and 1871:—

	Population.	Houses.
Census 1821	17,008	2,520
Census 1871	35,548	5,117

In 1795, the number of houses in Woolwich was only 1,200, and the population under 9,000 souls. The early growth of the population of Woolwich may be estimated by the comparison of the registers of baptisms and burials:—

	Baptisms.	Burials.
1680	72	98*
1730	125	158
1750	159	163
1760	161	186
1770	181	194
1780	262	285
1790	292	311
1795	357	390

* Representing a population of about 2,300.

In Parliament, Woolwich is represented as part of the Borough of Greenwich by two members, and it is also included in the County Division of West Kent, which has two members likewise.

THE ALMSHOUSES.

There are two groups of Almshouses in the parish, both, however, close together in the old part of the town. By far the oldest are those called the "Goldsmiths' Almshouses," which face Warren Lane, the ancient water-gate of the town, and a stone set in the front tells their history :—

"These Almshouses were endowed by Sir Martin Bowes, Knight, who was Lord Mayor of London in the year 1545, and were re-built by the Company of Goldsmiths, London, in the year 1771."

Tradition says that Sir Martin Bowes endowed the charity in gratitude for his son's life being saved by a Woolwich waterman, but we find by contemporary records that Sir Martin had valuable estates both at Woolwich and Plumstead, and, although this does not disprove the legend, it affords a reason for his feeling an interest in the locality, without seeking for an accidental one. The Goldsmiths' Company visit these almshouses once a year.

The Parochial Almshouses, as they are called, stand at the back of the Goldsmiths', with their front in Rope Yard Rails. They are on the site of the old workhouse, and when that establishment was broken up on the creation of the Greenwich Union, these houses were built, principally by the liberality of Mr. Thomas Clark, of Walworth, who formerly resided at Woolwich, and Miss Reed, of Woolwich Common. A small income is insured to the poor inmates by the money invested on behalf of the almshouses, the fund being as follows :—Mr. Thomas Clark's gift and bequest, £5,000 ; Miss Reed's bequest, £400; collected by the Board of Commissioners, £54 12s. 10d. ; invested by Mr. Thomas Morgan, £100 ; various private subscriptions, £446 13s. 10d. More funds are greatly needed, and we heartily commend the cause to the charitable.

We have been compelled, in order to put some limit on the dimensions of this chapter, to condense much of the matter, and omit altogether many details which might have been interesting, though not of paramount importance. Old residents have voluntarily, and with the greatest kindness, favoured us with information, part of which we have embodied in the foregoing history, but some of which we have been obliged to exclude. An excellent sample of these communications is that of a valued correspondent who encloses a copy of verses written to aid a bazaar which was held some fifty years ago on behalf of a fund to help the wives and families of soldiers gone abroad, and says :—"These were sold for the nominal sum of 6d. in aid of a fund raised by a penny subscription got up by the wife of one of the Royal Artillery Riding School officers, Lieut. Tanswell, assisted by her niece collecting, (a daughter of Quartermaster Mc Naghton, late Scot's Greys, who lies in Charlton Churchyard, near the road.) Of course the fund was very small, even aided by the unvarying kindness of the ladies of the corps, and they got up these bazaars, one of the leading spirits being the late Lady Strangways, of the Rocket Troop. At one of these fancy fairs held in Mrs Tanswell's Roughs, near Nightingale Vale, the then commandant, Lord Bloomfield, good naturedly *sold pies* at 2s. 6d. each, Mrs. Strangways having supplied his lordship with an apron and tray, (he was wearing the insignia of a G.C.B.,) she attending to take the cash, 'no change given,' or notice thereof either. A goodly sum was realised. The Artillery Band played in the adjacent grounds belonging to the late Sir E. Perrott, Bart. Nor was that the only benevolent act of Lord Bloomfield for the gunners' wives and children. He paid a large sum (probably in the whole £300) for building schools at the huts on the Common, as well as subscribing to and opening the National School in Woolwich, and promoting wash-houses for the soldiers' wives.

.   .   .   .   . The poet Wordsworth stayed at a house in Nightingale Vale many years since, and was much charmed by the locality and the sweet notes of Philomel. It is mentioned by him in his works. It is notable that the first lifeboat of the present National Institution was built by Mr. Peake, assistant master shipwright at Woolwich Dockyard. The Duke (Algernon) of Northumberland, came down to the launch, which took place from the great slip there. It was placed upon the large carriage built for it by .Col. Colquhoun, R.A., in the Arsenal, but as the beam was too large, the wheels had to be taken off to get it through the gates, and it was floated back to the Arsenal by the lifeboat. I remember the duke saying to me, ' All this is taking steps in the right direction ' We all thought it seemed. like perfection, but that was then a long way off."

We may add that we shall be happy to receive any information which will add to the accuracy and completeness of future editions of this work.

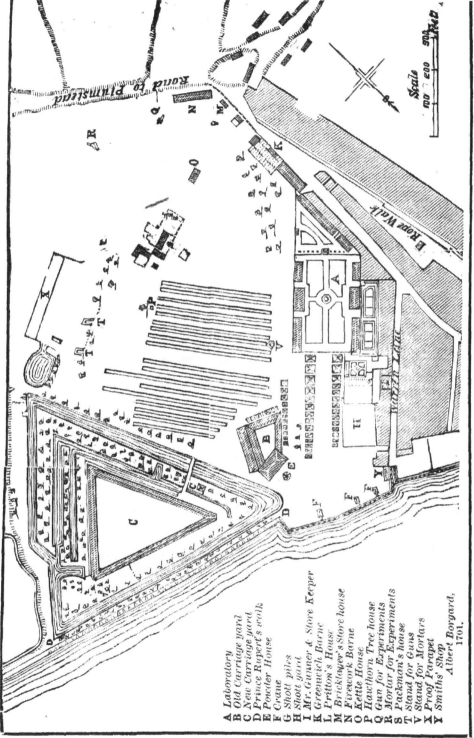

A Laboratory
B Old Carriage yard
C New Carriage yard
D Prince Rupert's walk
E Powder House
F Crane
G Shott piles
H Shott yard
I Mr. Gunner & Store Keeper
K Greenwich Barne
L Pritton's House
M Bricklayer's Store house
N Firework Barne
O Kettle House
P Hawthorn Tree house
Q Gun for Experiments
R Mortar for Experiments
S Packman's house
T Stand for Guns
V Stand for Mortars
X Proof Parapet
Y Smiths' Shop
Albert Borgard,
1701.

MAP OF WOOLWICH WARREN IN 1701, BY GENERAL BORGARD, R.A.

PRINCE RUPERT'S TOWER AND PALACE AT WOOLWICH
WARREN, 1684.

The Tower was demolished in 1786. The building, which is still standing, has since been the Royal Military Academy, and is now the Royal Laboratory and Pattern Room.

HISTORY OF THE ROYAL ARSENAL.

HE origin of the Royal Arsenal at Woolwich was long ascribed, not to native talent, but to the superior wit of a foreign mechanic, who, taking advantage of English blundering, contrived to establish the supremacy of his own wisdom.

Andrew Schalch bears an honoured name in Woolwich; his bones rest revered in our old churchyard, and his descendants have been amongst us to this day; but we cannot allow him to monopolise for ever the glory of having produced Woolwich Arsenal. Captain Grover, Royal Engineers, to whom belongs the credit of setting history right in this particular, says that he can trace the error back no farther than 1802*, and he discards it altogether.

The popular, but erroneous, tradition was to the following effect:—Young Schalch, a native of Schaffhausen, in Switzerland, happened to be travelling in England in 1716, according to the system adopted by his countrymen of getting experience (and sometimes profit) out of foreign lands. He was a journeyman founder, and he went to the foundry which the Government then had at Moorfields to see a great casting, which attracted many spectators, on the 10th of May in that year. Schalch, so says the story, noticed that the interior of the mould was damp, and warned Colonel Armstrong, the Surveyor of the Ordnance, that an explosion would be the consequence, advising him to retire from the spot. The Colonel did not believe the prediction, but cautiously kept at a distance, and when the explosion occurred (there is no doubt that it did occur) he was not hurt, but a number of the spectators were killed and wounded. A few days afterwards an advertisement appeared in the newspapers, inviting the young foreigner to present himself to the Government, which he did, and he was promptly commissioned to erect and take charge of another foundry, selecting the site himself. The spot he fixed upon was the Rabbit Warren at Woolwich, a place which he thought most suitable, as being near the river, for transport purposes—within a handy distance of London—and secure from invasion by sea; while there was also the advantage of having in the neighbourhood good loam for making the moulds.

All these advantages the place does, no doubt, possess; but, unfortunately for the legend, there are many and positive proofs that the Royal Arsenal existed, at least in embryo, long before 1716, and that its three great manufacturing departments, as we now find them—the Royal Laboratory, Royal Carriage Department, and Royal Gun Factories—had been already established when the accident at Moorfields led to the removal of the Brass Foundry to what was even then the Royal Arsenal, though bear-

* The story is told with great circumstance in the *European Magazine* of that year. We saw it repeated in a local newspaper as lately as February, 1875.

ing another name. Capt. Grover asserts, after much careful research, that no advertisement relating to Schalch can be found in any newspaper of the period, nor any allusion to his connection with the Moorfields explosion in any contemporaneous journal or public minute-book.

In fact, the Royal Arsenal has a history stretching back even as far as that of its sister establishment, the Dockyard, which we *know* was in existence in 1490, or thereabouts, when Henry VII. reigned. The probability is that the two originated about the same time, and that, besides being manufacturing establishments for the army and navy, they were also regarded as defences on the river for the protection of the Royal Palace at Greenwich, and of the Capital. One of the earliest references we have on the subject—Jordan's Parochial History of Enstone—speaks of the "remaines of the Armour at the Tower and Woolwich, A.D. 1603," and sets forth that there was still " at Woolwich, as in the former remaine taken, 3 backes and brests for almayne corsletts (besides 1 odd backe), 74 collers with bombards, 48 burgonets and buskins, 333 murrions blacke, and 12 burgonets, old and nothing worth." (*Backes* and *brests* were the suits of armour for the pikemen, or " corsletts"; *bombards* were padded breeches; and *burgonets* were helmets). We have no positive proof, it is true, that this depot was on the site of the present Arsenal,* but in a letter, still preserved, from King Charles II. to Prince Rupert, dated 13th June, 1667, the latter is ordered to take the direction of preparing certain works and batteries at or near Woolwich for the better security of the river against the Dutch fleet †; and there are other records extant showing that a 60-gun battery was built at Woolwich in the same year. Now, the oldest known plan of the Royal Warren, as it was then termed, is preserved at the Royal Military Repository, Woolwich (see page 108), and that is dated 1701, only 34 years later than the order to Prince Rupert; and it shows a parapet along the river front of the Arsenal 13 feet thick, and pierced with 40

---

* Lysons, writing in 1796, says that the Gun-wharf at Woolwich is a very ancient place, and formerly occupied the site of the Market-place in High Street. (See *Lyson's Environs of London*).

† In 1666, when the Dutch sailed up to Chatham, nine large ships were deliberately sunk in the river at Woolwich, and four at Blackwall, to obstruct the threatened advance of the audacious Dutchmen. (Hume's *History of England*).

embrasures—the other 20 guns might have been placed on the
parapet. This, we cannot doubt, was the battery erected by
Prince Rupert in 1667. In the rear of the parapet, the map
shows what is called " Prince Rupert's Walk," a footpath running
along the edge of the river, where the West Wharf now is,
having on the river side the parapet aforesaid, and on the other
hand a wet ditch or moat, which encloses in a triangular space
two or three acres of land (now Ordnance Store Department,
Shell Foundry, and part of the Gun Factories), within which
enclosure appears the " New Carriage Yard." The " Old
Carriage Yard " stood then on the site of the present Laboratory
offices, and the only buildings which seem to have kept their
ground until now are those of the Royal Laboratory itself, which
(though they have since been rebuilt) stood square and compact
as at this day. The old proof butt, which many of us remember
standing between the Gun Factories and the Canal, is shown in
this plan, and the range in front of it extends up to the very
doors of the Laboratory. In this interesting sketch, Beresford
Square, as we call it, appears to be a village green, with two or
three cottages upon it, a few more dotting the roadside along
Green's End ; and the only streets shown are those now known
as Cannon Row, Warren Lane, and Harden's Lane, which
appear exactly as we now find them. Plumstead Road was a
green lane, with a bye-way leading across the lower part of the
Arsenal towards the river, and the Arsenal itself was plentifully
studded with trees. This plan alone, which is signed by General
Borgard, one of the earliest and most distinguished officers of
the Royal Artillery, is sufficient to upset the 1716 theory.

A later plan, drawn by John Barker, in 1748, shows the old
brass foundry built as we now see it, and also the Dial Square,
which contained even until recently the whole of the apparatus
for boring and finishing the guns cast in the adjacent foundry.
The group of officers' quarters and offices near the present gates
are also marked on this map, having been erected during the
preceeding thirty years. The block, which faces north-east
(directly towards the river), is described as " The old Artillery
barracks and quarters," and the other block, at right angles,
facing the north-west, is called " the new Artillery barracks and
quarters." The Select Committee offices were then " the house

of Mr. Schalch." During the 47 years which elapsed between the production of General Borgard's plan and this one, the moat round the "Carriage Yard," down by the river, became partly filled in, its bridge had disappeared, and the carriage yard itself was nearly obliterated, its place being occupied by the "Storekeeper's Orchard," thus preparing the way for the subsequent creation on the same spot of the Storekeeper's Department, rechristened of late years in the name of Ordnance Store Department. A few more cranes and landing platforms appear on Barker's map, occupying the river face of the Laboratory Department, and "the Rookery," not long since disestablished, makes a green avenue between the Laboratory and the Dial Square.

Anxious not to weary the reader, we pass by a number of records, such as estimates for flooring storehouses at Woolwich, and making them " wind and water tite for ye keeping dry of ye powder match and other provisions," and a great number of references which crop up during the same century; mentioning only such as are requisite to give a succinct history of our subject.

The "Old Carriage Yard" before mentioned appears to have been built as early as 1682, and that it was not only a store but a factory is shown by a minute dated 1683, stating that Mr. Peach, the storekeeper broke up 89 condemned gun carriages and took out the iron work. In 1668 "all gun carriages and stores" were removed from Deptford to Woolwich, and it seems that the Laboratory before 1695 was at Greenwich. On the 3rd of December in that year, we find an order given to a certain William Edge to "fetch gravel and raise and level the ground for the new Laboratory at Woolwich, according to an agreement made with Mr. Boulter."

A thousand cannon and 10,000 cannon round shot were sent to Woolwich from the Tower in 1682, and two or three years later a "shot yard" was regularly established.

About this time the Arsenal began to be known as "Woolwich Tower Place," from Prince Rupert's Tower, which seems to have been erected before the Laboratory. In 1681 the Board of Ordnance acknowledged its liability to keep in repair the bank of the Thames at " the Tower Place, Woolwich;" and in 1684, Capt.

Leake, master gunner of England, who had a house at Woolwich Tower Place, was ordered to erect a wooden butt for the practice of artillery there.

We have now seen that the Laboratory and the Carriage Department existed, and that guns were proved here prior to 1684, but at this period all guns for the military and naval services were still made and supplied by private manufacturers, being always proved before acceptance sometimes at the Old Artillery Ground in Spitalfields, and sometimes at the New Artillery Ground at Moorfields. The proof of ordnance was, however, transferred to Woolwich sometime between 1665 and 1680, at which time Major Matthew Bayly (? Bagley) was "ye proof master," and George Browne, Esq., was "His Majesty's founder of brass and iron ordnance." It was not unusual to allow private founders to prove their guns at the Woolwich Tower Place, at their own cost, as is done to this day.

The Moorfields foundry, which has become part of our history through the explosion which occurred there, was taken by Mr. Matthew Bagley, in 1704, and for 12 years he cast brass guns and mortars for the Ordnance. The explosion took place on Thursday, the 10th of May, 1716. A number of guns, captured from the French by Marlborough, were ordered to be re-cast, and the interest created by the trophies and the fact of the casting being a large one, attracted a considerable number of people to the factory, which was in the City Road, near the present site of Finsbury Square. The catastrophe is reported thus in the *Mercurious Politicus* of May 18th, 1716:—

Several gentlemen were invited to see the metal run, which, being a very great and curious piece of art, a great many persons of quality came to see it, and some general officers of the army among the rest; but whether it was some unusual hindrance in the work, or their better fate, that occasioned the metal to be longer preparing than usual, we know not, but be that as it will, the gentlemen waiting till past ten o'clock, went all or most of them away. About eleven at night the metal being ready, was let go . . . . . the burning metal no sooner sunk down to the bottom of the mould, but with a noise and force equal to that of gunpowder, it came pouring up again, blowing like the mouth of a *Vulcano* or a little *Vesuvius*. There was in the place about 20 men, as well workmen as spectators, 17 of whom were so burnt that nothing more horrible can be thought of, neither can words describe their misery. About 9 of the 17 are already dead, the other 8 are yet living, but in such a condition that the surgeons say they have very small hopes of above 2 of them.

The *Flying Post* of the 12th May, 1716, says:—

'Tis generally agreed that this sad accident was owing to the dampness of the mould.

An autibiography of General Borgard, preserved in the Royal Artillery Library at Woolwich, contains the following account of this accident:—

On our arrivall at London I was order'd by the Board of Ordnance to lay before them tables and draughts of all natures of brass & iron cannon, mortars, &c., which was done accordingly, & approved of. After the said draughts 2 twenty-four pounder brass cannon were order'd to be cast by Mr. Bagley in his foundry at Windmill Hill (Moorfields), at the casting of which I was ordered to be present. In the Founding, the mettall of one of the guns blowed into the air, burnt many of the spectators, of which seventeen dy'd out of 25 persons, & myself received 4 wounds.

Besides General Borgard, Mr. George Harrison, Superintendent of the Foundries, and several other officials were burnt, and amongst the killed were Mr. Hall, Clerk of the Ordnance, Mr. Bagley the founder, and his son.

The result was the establishment of the brass foundry at the Woolwich Tower Place, or Arsenal, which, as we have shown had existed for, perhaps, a hundred years before—in some form or other. In the Tower records of June 19th, 1716, is the following minute:—

It having for many yeares been the Opinion of the most experienced Officers that the Government should have a Brass Foundery of their own, and whereas Mr. Bagley's Foundery is the only own for Casting Brass Ordnance and lyable to dangerous Accidents wch cant be prevented. It is therefore order'd that a Proposal and Estimate be made for Building a Royal Brass Foundery at His Majesty's Tower Place at Woolwich, & the Charge thereof Defrayed out of the £5000 given this Year by Parliament for recasting Brass Ordnce & yt no time be lost herein, inasmuch as there are but 2 12-Pounders, and not 1 18 or 24-Pounder for Land Service. A Letter to Mr. Henry Lidgbird to attend the Surveyr Genl the 20th about providing Bricks for the Royal Brass Foundery at Woolwich.

The "most experienced officers," having obtained this authority, which they had probably been long seeking, for reforms of this kind are always slow, set to work with such promptitude that within two months £300 was ordered to be paid for bricklayer's work at the new Brass Foundry at Woolwich; and on the 10th July, 1716, the *London Gazette* contained an advertisement, as follows:—

Whereas a Brass Foundery is now building at Woolwich for his Majesty's service, all Founders as are desirous to cast Brass Ordnance are to give in their Proposals forthwith, upon such terms as are regulated by the Principal Officers of His Majesty's Ordnance, which may be seen at their Office in the Tower.

Mr. Andrew Schalch then appears upon the scene, and in August, 1716, we find an order that, if enquiries proved satisfactory, he should be employed in building the furnaces and providing utensils for the Royal Foundry, at a salary of £5 per day. In October, the British Minister at Brussels reported that the references as to "Mr. Schalk" were satisfactory, that he bore a good character at Doway, and was an able founder; and, accordingly, he was appointed at £5 per diem, dating from the 20th of September. The little bit of romance associated with his appointment may have had some foundation, but it lacks proof. Andrew Schalch, however. was for 60 years master-founder at Woolwich, and honoured be his memory. He died at Charlton, in 1776, aged 84 years, and he was buried in Woolwich churchyard, on the Dockyard side. Five of his descendants have served in the Royal Artillery, and his name has seldom been without a representative at Woolwich.

The Brass Foundry, the same building we now see, was said to have been designed by Sir John Vanbrugh. A modern writer has described it as "stately, solemn, and picturesque," "with its high-pitched roof, red brickwork, and carved porch, looking like a fine old gentleman amid the factory ranges which, within these few years have sprung up around. It is impossible (says the same writer) to contemplate this building without respect, "for forth from its portals have issued that victorious ordnance which since the days of George II., has swept the battle grounds of the old and new worlds."

The south portion of the Dial Square was built about the same time, but the present erection on that site is clearly of more modern date. The growth of the Royal Arsenal was gradual and almost continuous during the 18th century, but it was reserved for the last fifty years* (so full of progress in all branches of science) to quadruple the size and increase one hundredfold the

---

* The Departmental account books show that in 1836, the total number of men employed in the Royal Gun Factories (then the Inspector of Artillery's Department) was only 46.

resources of the vast establishment, and make it what we now find it—unequalled throughout the world.

Prince Rupert's Tower,* adjoining the Laboratory, was pulled down in August, 1786. The building which remains is still known by tradition as "Prince Rupert's Palace," but it is considered doubtful if it was ever the residence of Prince Rupert, though he had much to do at the "Warren"; and, as the Arsenal bore the name of Tower Place about his time, it is not unreasonable to suppose that he either erected the building, or found it standing. That part of the building which is now the Laboratory pattern-room was rebuilt by Sir John Vanbrugh in 1719, and is said to have been first used as offices, but the size of its apartments and its external appearance, are evidences that it was meant for some higher purpose. In 1741, we find it converted, by order of George II., into an instruction room for Cadets intended to serve as officers in the Royal Artillery and Engineers, thus establishing the nucleus of the Royal Military Academy. (See note, page 68.) The hoppers of the rain-water pipes still bear the date of rebuilding " G.R., 1719."

Thus we have seen that the Ordnance Corps—the germ of the Royal Artillery and Royal Engineers—the great Garrison of Woolwich, and the Royal Military Academy, as well as the Manufacturing Departments, all had their origin within the walls of the Royal Arsenal. The buildings which we have pointed out as the " old and new Barracks," also bear on some of their water pipes the date of 1719.

The old newspapers contain frequent references to the Royal Warren. In April, 1756 (on the outbreak of the seven years' war), we learn that " the old chapel in the Warren at Woolwich is filled with bombs, grape-shot, chain, and double-headed shot, ready to be embarked at a minute's warning;" and in April, 1757, appears an order to the Cadets at the Academy, directing that " the first Cadet that is found swimming in the Thames shall be taken out naked and put in the guard-room."

The following paragraph relates to what appears to be the first recorded Royal visit to the Arsenal (though Royalty was

---

* For sketch of this building, see page 109. A reference to the ancient map of the Arsenal, at page 108, will show that Rupert's Walk, in 1701, extended almost in a line from this building, and a few old trees which stand in front of the Royal Gun Factories probably mark the extremity of the avenue, and point out the direction it took.

often at the Dockyard), and it gives an interesting idea of the time, the place, and the people. The date is 9th July, 1772, and the King spoken of is, of course, George III. :—

On Tuesday last the King arrived at this place (Woolwich). At a little before 10 in the morning his Majesty entered the Warren (pre-ceeded by 24 rope-makers* dressed in white with round hats deco-rated by ribbons, who had run before his Majesty's carriage from Blackheath) attended by a party of the light horse. His Majesty stepped out of his carriage, and was received by Lord Townsend, as Master-General of the Ordnance, on the Parade, when he was saluted by a discharge of 21 twelve-pounders. The guard rested their arms, and the drums and music beat the march ; the royal standard was displayed on the mortar battery, and every window filled with ladies. His Majesty passed in front of the old invalids and the guard, to the new-erected foundery, where Mr. Van Bruggen shewed His Majesty the various progressions of casting brass guns, such as the preparation of the clay, forming the moulds, fixing the trunnions, and the motion of the fire in the furnaces, occasioned by the subterraneous galleries that convey an uncommon blast of wind from every quarter. The King then entered the boring room, for boring guns cast solid, by an horizontal boring machine, extremely curious and well contrived, (likewise the work of Mr. Van Bruggen) where a 42-pounder was bored in his Majesty's presence. From the foundery his Majesty went through the gun-walk to the mortar battery, and saw several shells thrown from mortars of various diameters, both for land and sea service ; some ricochet granadoes were likewise thrown from howit-zers. From thence his Majesty went to the Royal Military Academy, where he saw a very curious model of a fortification, together with the lines of approach, parallels, and saps, explained in a very military-like manner by the inspector of the Academy, Captain Smith, who is said to have been twelve years in the Prussian service. His Majesty then viewed the drawings and other exercises of the Upper Academy, explained by Dr. Pollock, Professor of Artillery and Fortification ; after which he returned into the grand room of the Academy, and was regaled with a breakfast and repast.

It was on the occasion of a second Royal visit to Woolwich that the great national establishment received its present name. On the 9th of April, 1805, George III., accompanied by the Queen and Princesses, came down to the Warren, the inappro-priate title of which appears to have struck his Majesty for the first time. Accordingly an order appeared in the June fol-lowing, in these words :—

The Ordnance Board have signified to General Lloyd who com-mands the Artillery at Woolwich, that the *Warren* at that place is

---

* The Government Rope-yard was outside the Royal Arsenal, and a separate establishment.

no longer to bear that name ; but from this time to be denominated the " Royal Arsenal !" The old name had its origin from the place having actually been a *rabbit warren*, but the name of one of the tamest of all animals was certainly ill-suited to the nature of the place. On the recent Royal visit to what is called the Warren, where all ordnance, stores, ammunition, &c., are lodged, his Majesty noticed how little appropriate the name was to the place, and suggested the propriety of changing it to that of " Arsenal." The Master General admitted the justice of the idea, and instantly adopted it ; henceforward, therefore, in compliment to his Majesty's suggestion, the Warren is to be called "The Royal Arsenal."

The word is said to be derived from the Roumaunt *Arthenal*, a " citadel," or, more strictly, a " naval citadel."

In 1796, according to " Environs of London," published in that year, the number of artificers and labourers (exclusive of convicts) employed in the various departments of Woolwich Warren, was about 1,500, including 300 boys ; and that the making of canvas bags for the use of the Warren, furnished employment for a great number of poor women in the town.

THE CONVICTS' BURIAL GROUND

was originally on the site of the Royal Gun Factories, and their remains were found in considerable quantities when the Rifled Ordnance Factory was erected in 1859. They were re-buried behind the proof-butts, where a new graveyard for the poor sinners had been for some years established.

Hastily drawing this too-long chapter to a conclusion, we may remark that the extension of the wharf from the Laboratory eastward to the coal dock was carried out in 1809-11, and that the various buildings in the Military Store Department and the present Carriage Square, came into being about the same period. The Carriage Square was then strictly speaking " a square," whose boundaries are still well defined, though the department has far outgrown its original limits. For many years afterwards, the space now occupied by the Cap Factory, Mounting Ground, Shell Factory, and Gun Factories, remained open from the Laboratory Gates down to the old proof-butt, which stood in a reed swamp close by a large pond. The convicts, who then inhabited the hulks moored at the Royal Arsenal, filled up this swamp with mud scraped from the river shore and the debris brought from the excavations at the making of St. Katharine's Docks. Convict hulks (Warrior, Justitia, and others) were moored at the Dockyard as well as the Arsenal, and the prisoners were employed at hard labour on most of the public works at Woolwich. It used to be a painful sight to see the poor wretches driven through the streets, to and from their work, in gangs of a score or so, attached to a single chain. The hulks were finally removed from Woolwich in 1856, the year which ended the Crimean war, and one marked at the Royal Arsenal by the opening of the T pier, where the first of the troops landed on their return to Woolwich.

The Royal Arsenal consists of 333 acres, independent of that occupied by powder-magazines in the marshes. Less than one-sixth of the area is in the parish of Woolwich, the remainder is within the boundary of Plumstead.

Its greatest development took place in the years just prior to 1860, when the Royal Laboratory was rebuilt and extended, and the Cap Factory, Shell Foundry, Gun Factories, and many other buildings erected, to supply the demand for war material of increased power and in larger quantities, which had arisen through the War with Russia. These events belong to modern times, and we do not propose to deal with current history in this place. The principal incidents connected with the Arsenal in its modern days, will, however, be found recorded in our Chronology of Woolwich.

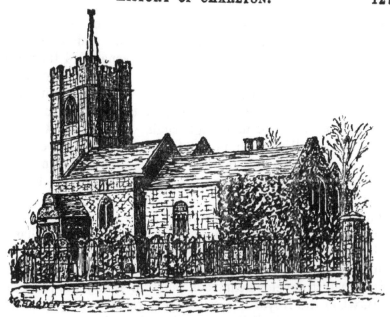

OLD CHARLTON CHURCH.

CHARLTON.

:o:

HARLTON Village, in which is comprised the oldest and best part of the parish, is beautifully situated on rising ground overlooking the Thames and the country beyond. The derivation of its name seems easily traced, for *ceorl*, or *churl* in Saxon and Old English means husbandman, and *tone* is but a step from *town*. Charlton, therefore, was, in the Saxon era, the "town of husbandmen," as it is in a great measure to this day. Its principal ornament is the old and handsome building known as Charlton House, the seat of the Baronets of the Wilson family, and Lords of the Manor of Charlton and Woolwich. The building was erected about 1610, during the reign of James I.,

I

and is enclosed in a park and pleasure grounds of about 70 acres. The arched gateway standing on the lawn marks the former boundary. The remainder of the enclosure before the house is said to have been open common, and the Fair used to be held upon it. The interior of the house comprises a noble hall, in which the modern baronets have occasionally permitted public meetings of the inhabitants for charitable, patriotic, and political purposes; a private chapel in the north-east corner, and some splendid apartments, in one of which is a fine chimney piece, of black marble, in which, once upon a time, it is said that Lord Downe saw the reflection of a robbery committed on Blackheath, and it is added that he sent his servants who captured the thieves. The house was built by Sir Adam Newton, who was preceptor to Prince Henry, son of James I., and the young Prince (who died at the age of eighteen) and his brother Charles (afterwards King Charles I.) spent a great portion of their youth here. The ceiling of one of the rooms is still decorated with the Royal Arms and the Plumes of the Prince of Wales; and as lately as 1807, Charlton has been a Royal residence. We are told in that year that Her Royal Highness the Princess of Wales, who lived in the old house, recently replaced by two new ones, near St. Paul's Church, made it her constant country residence, and that she was much beloved in the neighbourhood.

CHARLTON OLD CHURCH.

The old parish church is dedicated to St. Luke, and is said to have been surrendered to the Crown with the manor of Charlton at the dissolution of the monasteries in the reign of Henry VIII., (1537), being at that time one of the possessions of the monastery of St. Saviour, Bermondsey. It remained vested in the Crown until the reign of James I., who granted it to Sir Adam Newton, at whose death it was, by his desire, greatly improved, being for the greater part re-erected and beautified within and without. The patronage continued in the hands of the Lord of the Manor of Charlton until 1714, when Sir William Langhorn gave it to the Rector, Robert Warren, from whom it descended by purchase and by natural succession for many generations. There are some very ancient monuments in the church, and many personages of high distinction in history lie buried in its precincts.

A bust by Chantrey is to be seen in the church with an inscription to the memory of the Right Hon. Spencer Perceval, who, in 1812, while Prime Minister, was assassinated by a lunatic named Bellingham. It is remarkable that in the same churchyard are the remains of Edward Drummond, private secretary to Sir Robert Peel, for whom he was mistaken when murdered by McNaughten. He was brother of the Rev. Arthur Drummond, rector of Charlton, and brother-in-law of Sir T. Maryon Wilson, Lord of the Manor.*

The new church of St. Paul is a much grander edifice, and was erected a few years ago when the parish was divided into two ecclesiastical districts, each having a rector of its own. The schools in connection with this church are situated in the Lower part of the parish, a district of comparatively recent growth, and for the most part unfavourably built below the water-line in the marshes.

Charlton was formerly famed for its annual revel called Horn Fair, which was held on the 18th October (St. Luke's day) and the two days following. It dated, according to tradition, from the time of King John, but it was eventually happily extinguished at the earnest wish of the inhabitants, the last fair being held in 1871.†

The population of Charlton and the Liberty of Kidbrook, which is included in the same district for registration purposes, is about 12,000. This district comprises an area of 1,986 acres. In 1821 there were only seven dwellings in Kidbrook, and 73 inhabitants. It is now a populous and wealthy place. Charlton in 1821 contained only 394 houses and 1,626 souls.

The Cemetery at Charlton is a beautiful spot, and is kept in excellent order. Visitors are free to enter and walk about the grounds every day. The ancient road from Charlton Ferry to Shooters' Hill passed along the northern end of this cemetery, connecting Hanging Wood and Woolwich Common.

---

* In the bend of the lane, opposite the churchyard, stood formerly the Cage and the Stocks.

† A history of Charlton without the equivocal and probably mendacious story of "King John and the Miller," and without a description of Horn Fair, is confined to this work; but, seeing that these two subjects and the legend of the vision in the fireplace have been repeated over and over again *ad nauseum*, the circumstance ought to be a grateful one.

Hanging Wood, which is still a large and picturesque piece of woodland, formerly stretched from the Fairfield to what we now call Frances Street, Woolwich, and from the Lower Road to the Barrack Field. A footpath ran through it from Woolwich to Charlton, and it was intersected in the other direction by the road just mentioned to Shooters' Hill, traces of which we may still find. Mr. J. Hewitt, the historian, who resided for several years in Wood Street, and has rescued from oblivion many interesting records respecting the neighbourhood, has traced the former boundaries of Hanging Wood with much exactness. He starts from the corner of Charlton Lane and the Lower Road, and makes the circuit of its site eastward, as follows:—Pursuing the Lower Road eastward to within about a hundred yards of the "Lord Howick" tavern, which stands at the south west corner of the Dockyard, then with a sweep to the south-east, passing by the railroad foot-bridge and the top of Prospect Place, we approach the west corner of the Marine Barracks, overpassing Godfrey Street a few yards. From this point we make a straight line, taking in the oak trees of the garden of "Rosemount" (east of Pellipar Road) over the "Green Hill" to the Observatory. From here another straight line runs to about the middle of the wall of Charlton Cemetery; a bend to the north-west, now brings us to the corner of Charlton Park; then along the high road to Charlton village, round the Fair-field, by St. Paul's church, along the bank of great trees running first northward and then more to the east, and finally striking the Greenwich road at or near the toll-gate from which we started.*

The old gravel-pits in rear of Woodland Terrace have apparently furnished "road materials" for many generations. They constitute a favourite resort of geologists, the strata being very clearly marked. This was at the edge of the wood, and on the top of the cliff are evident remains of an ancient camp, probably a Roman entrenchment, or the ruder fortifications of the Ancient Britons.

Hanging Wood in the old days was the scene of frequent crimes. We find the following among the old records preserved in the British Museum:—

---

* See old map, page 108.

1732.—On Sunday morning the Rev. Mr. Richardson, going from Lewisham to preach at Woolwich, was attacked by a foot-pad in Hanging Wood, who robbed him of a guinea, leaving him but two-pence, and then made off.

1762.—Several people have been robbed this week in Hanging Wood, near Woolwich.

1782.—Three men robbed a boatswain of a man-of-war, near Hanging Wood, of his watch and ten guineas, but some gentlemen coming up they took to the wood, &c.

1812.—On Tuesday last a poor boy was murdered in a wood near Woolwich by a ruffian who, having robbed his master and being pursued, fled for refuge to the wood ; where, being seen by the boy, the latter screamed with terror of him, on which the villain seized and strangled him. He was apprehended soon after, when he confessed that he was nearly three hours perpetrating the horrid deed.

The lane in rear of the Camp and cottages on the Common was the old high road to London. It used to pass through the grounds of Charlton Park, entering where there is now a gate, and emerging at the other old gateway in Marlborough Lane, and so on to Shooters' Hill Road and Blackheath. The road is still to be traced throughout its entire length (see map of 1778, page 102). Speaking of the cottages, Mr. Hewitt says, " They were built in replacement of a number of mud huts which had been run up by soldiers who did not like barrack quarters. An old inhabitant of the neighbourhood states that he well remembers these mud huts, that they reached far up the Common, and that there were several hundreds of them." Owing to an outbreak of diphtheria among the soldiers' children inhabiting these huts, they were vacated in March, 1875, and subsequently demolished.

BHURTPOOR GUN ON WOOLWICH COMMON.

ST. MARGARET'S CHURCH, PLUMSTEAD.

PLUMSTEAD.

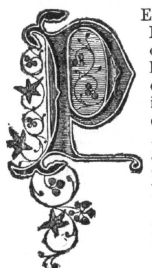

ERHAPS the most remarkable thing about Plumstead is its sudden growth and rapid development from a mere hamlet into a large and populous town. Between the censuses of 1851 and 1861, the number of inhabitants was more than trebled, the increase being from 8,000 to upwards of 24,000, and the population now is fully 30,000. Nearly all Burrage Town (as the western end is called), and, in fact, half the houses in the parish (of which there are about 5,000) were built in the years 1854—60. In 1800 there were only 214 houses in the whole of Plumstead, consisting merely of a cluster near the old village church, another nest of cottages at Cole Fields (now absorbed in the Royal Arsenal) nearly opposite the Dover Castle—having the old road-side inn called by that name at the corner—and a few others scattered about the farms and gardens.

Tracing back to the earliest records, we find by Domesday Book that in William the Conqueror's time the Abbot of St. Augustin's had the manor of "Plumstede," which was taxed at "two sulings and one yoke," and that in the demesne there was "one carnucate and 17 villiens with 6 cottagers," and "a wood for the pannage of 5 hogs." Of Burrage Town, we may explain that it derives its name from an old family that owned the land, but the name of the family has been corrupted strangely, even in recent times. It was in the reign of Edward III., 1330, the property of de Burghesh, of Norman descent; and Burwash Court, the family seat, was in existence during the early part of the present century. It was then known as "Burrish Place," and the situation of the mansion was that occupied by the houses at the bottom of Burrage Road, called "Burrage Place" to this day. The freehold has descended to the Pattison family. In the old vestry-books we read that in March, 1770, was buried "Mrs. Mary Pattison, from Burwash." The gradual transition of "Burghesh"—through "Burwash" and its shorter sound "Burrish"—down to "Burrage," affords an interesting illustration of the mutability of names. An old work called "Kent Surveyed and Illustrated," by Thomas Phillipots, published in 1659, has the following, under the head of "Plumstede" :—

Burwash Court is an eminent seat in this parish, made more illustrious by being wrapped up in the revenue of the noble family of Burghest or Burwash. Bartholomew de Burghest died possessed of it in the 28th year of Edward 3rd (Rot. Exe. w. 38), and left it to his son Bartholomew, Lord Burwash, who, in the 43rd year of the above said Prince, conveyed it with much other land to Sir Walter de Pavely, Knight of the Garter, in which family it continued until the reign of Richard 2nd, and then it was alienated to William Chickley, Alderman of London, who left it to his son, John Chickley, by whose daughter and heir, Agnes, it came to be possessed by Mr. Tattershall, of Well Hall, in Eltham, who about the beginning of Henry 6th conveyed it to Boughton, in the descendent of which family it had a permanent abode until the age that our remembrance had an aspect on, and then it was passed away to Rowland Wilson, of London, and he upon his late decease gave it to his daughter and her heirs, who was first matched to Doctor Crisp, and now secondly to Colonel Row, of Hackney.

In 1702 the Crisp family sold the estate to Nathaniel Maxey, of London, merchant, and in the deed is described, " All that the manor or capital messuage commonly called or known by the

name of Burwash, Burrough Ashe, or Borage, with the appur-
tenances, containing about 300 acres." About the same time
James Pattison married Miss Mary Maxey, daughter of the above
Nathaniel Maxey, and thus it came into the Pattison family.
James Pattison died 22nd March, 1761, aged 85; and his son,
Nathaniel Pattison, died 22nd April, 1784, aged 70. The next
lineal descendant was Nathaniel Maxey Pattison, of Congleton,
Cheshire, whose only son was James Pattison, M.P., of London,
merchant, and he died 1849, aged 63. The estate under his
will is a family settlement.

Formerly the parish was unhealthy, but drainage and other
improvements have quite altered its character in that, as in other,
respects, and the mortality returns show that it can favourably
compare with any other place in England. Situated on the
gentle slope rising up from the river's edge to the summit of
Shooters' Hill, it has many natural advantages, and the beauties
of its scenery, especially from such spots as Shrewsbury Lane,
the north-eastern extremity of Plumstead Common, and the
rugged heights of Bostol Heath, cannot be equalled anywhere
within the same distance from London.

There are 3,388 acres in the parish of Plumstead, and from
its two extremities at Shooters' Hill and Crossness Point there is
a stretch of nearly five miles. It has two reaches of the river
Thames on its boundaries, but all the water frontage belongs to
the Government. There is, however, a public footpath along the
river wall.

We have elsewhere (page 76) dwelt on the certainty that
before this wall was built the river overflowed the marshes, and
we have no doubt that the present irregular line of the Plumstead Road marks the ancient strand or beach, in evidence of
which there is " Strand Place," in the Village.

OLD PLUMSTEAD CHURCH

is by no means a handsome building, but if we cannot admire it
for its beauty, we may reverence it for its great antiquity. It
was in all probability built originally at the time of the Normans,
and the walls on the south and west sides, with their narrow
lancet windows, now bricked up, are believed to be some 900
years old. The Rev. J. K. Walpole has pointed out a remark-

able stone in the pavement of the church, having an inscription round the edges, which, he thinks, from the characters employed, was engraved before the arrival of William the Conqueror. The tower and roofs were erected in the reign of Charles II., by Mr. Gossage, who is buried under the church. An inscription on his gravestone before the altar states that he caused the church to be repaired "after above twenty years lying waste and ruinous." The north aisle was rebuilt in 1820, and within the last few years the church has been further restored by uncovering the ancient pavement and the bases of the stone columns, which lay buried three feet deep in the "dust of ages." The building is said to have been at one time much larger, and its foundations have been traced in a north-easterly direction. It is not unreasonable to suppose that it was at first attached to a monastery, and that when the monastery disappeared the church only remained. It probably extended to the edge of the lane or manorway on the east side, and was half surrounded by the Thames at high-water, its elevated situation protecting it from the flood.

The old churchyard, into which the remains of generations of Plumstead men and women were crowded, raising it, Mr. Walpole says, several feet higher than its original level, was closed by an Order in Council, in Nov. 1860, when a meadow of $2\frac{1}{2}$ acres, to the south, was added to it, and is being rapidly covered with graves. Many brave officers and other distinguished men have found a quiet resting place in this old churchyard, alongside the humble and forgotten villagers. The old registers still preserved date back to a period when surnames were in their infancy. We are told that "Richard the Cobbler" was buried in 1690; that "Great Betty" was interred in 1744; and that "John the Taylor" was put to earth in 1747. Here is a puzzling record :—"1688. John Robards and Geo. Robards both died in one hole of a grenado shell, and was buried the 24th day of June." Among the tombs in the churchyard are some handsome and imposing ones, but the most remarkable epitaph is the following, which may be seen on the right of the footpath going towards Abbey Wood :—

James Darling, died 23rd July, 1812, aged 10 years.

> Weep not for me, my parents Dear
> There is no Witness wanted here.
> The hammer of Death was given to me
> For eating the Cherris off the tree.
> Next moning Death was to me so sweet
> My blised Jesus for to meet.
> He did ease me of my pain
> And i did join his holy train.
> The cruel one his death can't shun,
> For he must go when his glass is run.
> The horrows of Death 'isue to meet
> And tak his trial at the Judgment Seat.

The brief facts of the tragedy, here recorded, are that this little Darling, who was a cartridge boy in the Arsenal, was caught stealing cherries in an orchard, somewhere near the spot where the Queen's Arms stands in Burrage Road, and died next day, as alleged, from the punishment he then received. His captor was tried and acquitted for lack of a witness to prove the charge, but the dissatisfied friends of the youth devised this novel method of stinging him with an epitaph.

The Manor and Church of Plumstead, with the chapel of Wickham annexed, were, after the dissolution of the monasteries, granted by the King, in exchange for other estates, to Sir Edward Boughton, of Burwash Court, Plumstead; and his descendant, John Michel, of Richmond, devised, in 1685 the property to the provost and scholars of Queen's College, Oxford, who exercise still the privileges of Lord of the Manor.

Suffolk Place Farm was an estate belonging to the Duke of Suffolk in the reign of Henry the Eighth.

The hillock on Plumstead Common, between the Slade and the descent to Wickham Lane, was formerly the butt at which the artillerymen of the last century practised with their guns and mortars. There is an old drawing in the Royal Artillery Institution, in which a party is seen practising here at a range of about half a mile, their mortars standing on the opposite side of the Slade ravine.

The old Plumstead workhouse was close by the Slade, and is now Winn's Cottages. Agnes Place, Cage Lane, was also at one time the parish Workhouse, with the Cage and the Stocks close by. The old Vicarage House in the Village is now the Volunteer Tavern.

The old map which we publish at Page 102, shows several old roads in the parish which have now partly disappeared but may still be traced. On the south side of Jolly's meadow, behind the Slade Cottages, and, again further to the eastward, are to be seen sections of roadway which tradition says are parts of the old Roman road from London to the " Roman Docks" at Abbey Wood,* but the statement must be received with caution. The land in this and other parts of the parish became vested in the London Clothworkers' Company in the reign of Henry VIII., and so remains.

St. Margaret's Church, on Plumstead Common, was erected and constituted the parish church under the rectorship of the Rev. W. Acworth, who succeeded Mr. Shackleton in 1853. It is a very handsome and commodious edifice.

We do not profess to give the origin of the name this parish bears, for authorities differ, and we are inclined to doubt them all. Some say it was named after its plum trees, and others after the plumes or feathers obtained from the wild geese and herons in the marshes for the manufacture of pens. All we know is that it has borne the same name, with little orthographical variation, from time immemorial.†

The new Workhouse and Infirmary of the Woolwich Union, which occupy a prominent position in Plumstead village, belong rather to the present day than to history. We may briefly say that they were completed in 1873, and cost altogether nearly £30,000. They are considered models of their kind.

---

* See page 80.

† Weever, rector of Lesnes and Erith, 1631, in his "Funeral Monuments," says, under the head of "Plumsted," "Here under a faire gravestone lieth buried John Plumsted, Esquire, receiver general of the Dutchie of Laancaster." Weever also describes Sir Richard Lucy's tomb, which then stood in the chancel at Lesnes Abbey.

Sevendroog Castle

SHOOTERS' HILL.

O much has been written of Shooters' Hill that its history belongs to the nation rather than the locality. Nevertheless, a book about Woolwich would be incomplete which did not include something concerning the famous hill. We need not repeat the descriptions which have been so often given of the royal shooting parties in the days of Henry VIII., from which it probably derived its name, nor tell of the wonderful road over its summit which the Romans made. Speaking of its more recent history, we may say that the little thoroughfare now called Red Lion Lane was the main road from

Woolwich to Shooters' Hill, the present road up the Common being, until recent times, a mere track over the sward. What we call Constitution Hill was the nearest way to Eltham, and its continuation through the grounds about Severndroog Castle has been closed only within the last few years. The other way through the wood from near the "Bull" at the summit, has had its beauty entirely destroyed by an ugly close fence on each side, but nobody has dared to stop it. There is still one lovely ramble left us through the wood to Halfway-street, but it should be taken in fine weather, as the ground is inclined to softness.

The "Bull" was a large hotel in the coaching times, before the railways came and destroyed half the romance of the road. It stretched to the corner of Shrewsbury Lane, and was the first post-house at which travellers stopped *en route* from London to the Continent. Tradition says that Dick Turpin, the famed highwayman, frequented the road, and natives allege that it was at the "Bull" he put the landlady on the fire in order to make her confess where she had hidden her gold. A large stone stands beside the house, from which travellers used to mount their horses, and the neighbours insist on calling it "Turpin's stone." Robberies and murders hereabout were frequent in the "good old times," and it is within living memory that criminals have been hanged on the hill by the half-dozen together, and gibbetted afterwards. Lord Byron has vividly described an encounter with footpads at Shooters' Hill in one of his cantos, and the old newspapers record many such adventures. For instance, a paragraph in 1773, says:—

On Sunday night about 10 o'clock, Colonel Craige and his servant were attacked near Shuters' Hill by two highwaymen well mounted, who on the Colonel's declaring he would not be robbed, immediately fired and shot the servant's horse in the shoulder. On this the footman discharged a pistol, and the assailants rode off with great precipitation.

Another paragraph relates that the remains of some unfortunate traveller were once found in the wood lashed to a tree in the depths of the wood, where he had probably died of starvation. We also read that when the Princess Charlotte was residing at Shrewsbury House for her education, her tutor, Dr. Watson, had to obtain from the Shooters' Hill robbers leave for her Royal Highness to pass to and from London.

The last execution at Shooters' Hill was in the year 1809, when two labourers named Russell and Webb, who resided in what was termed the black houses, in the rear of the Hare and Billet Inn, at Blackheath, were hanged for highway robbery. They had been the terror of the whole neighbourhood for some years, committing several robberies both in mansions and on the highway. The gallows stood a little above the present position of the Fire Brigade Station, and the culprits were buried near the cross roads from Woolwich Common to Eltham. Fifty years afterwards their bones were discovered in excavating for the Police Station.

Severndroog Castle, which stands with its tower peering above the wood, was erected as an affectionate memorial by the widow of Sir William James, a gallant officer, who in 1775 captured a robber-fortress of that name in India. There is a fine view from the summit, but it is difficult to obtain admission, and even the road which led past it is now barred by a gate. The castle was built 1784.

The following verse was written by Bloomfield :—

> This far-seen monumental tower
>   Records the achievements of the brave,
> And Angria's subjugated power
>   Who plundered on the Eastern wave.

Bloomfield, the rural poet, enjoyed some sweet repose at Shooters' Hill, from whence he writes :—

> O'er eastern uplands, gay or rude
>   Along to Erith's envied spire,
> I start with strength and hope renewed,
>   And cherish life's rekindling fire.
>
> Now measure vales with straining eyes,
>   Now trace the churchyard's humble names ;
> Or climb brown heaths, abrupt that rise
>   And overlook the winding Thames.

The " brown heaths" are the commons at Plumstead and Bostol Hill.

The height of Shooters' Hill, at a point near the " Bull Inn" is 424 feet 6 inches above high water (Ordnance datum).

The conformation and situation of Shooters' Hill may be said to have determined the physical character of the whole district. From the water's edge, or what was once the water's edge, the ground rises gradually all the way to the top of the hill, and there is no doubt that the same reason which led the ancients to select London for the site of a town, attracted the early inhabitants of Woolwich—namely, a dry situation close to the river. It must be remembered that there were then broad shallows skirting the channel of the river on either side, and a landing place situate as Woolwich must have been, where the foot of this beautiful hill dipped in the stream, was no mean advantage to its fishermen. The convoluted sides of the hill as it descends through Woolwich are due to the same cause, the receding flood having formed seven valleys, which radiate towards the Thames, through Charlton, Woolwich, and Plumstead, undulating the surface in picturesque form, and creating a natural drainage of immense sanitary value. These seven valleys may be traced in the following situations :—1. Hanging Wood "Swamp"; 2. Prospect Row and Hill Street, continuing to the "Seven Sisters" on the Barrack Field; 3. St. Mary Street; 4. Brookhill Road; 5. Vicarage Park, Plumstead; 6. The Slade; 7. Wickham Lane. From the course taken by the present boundary line of Woolwich parish it is a reasonable conjecture that it was originally bounded on the east by the "Brook Hill" brook, and on the West by the Seven Sisters or Hill Street valley, and the stream which occupied its bed.

SHOOTERS' HILL CHURCH AND SCHOOL.

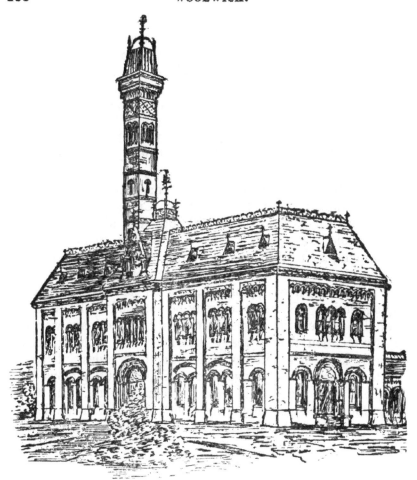

CROSSNESS PUMPING STATION.

THE MAIN DRAINAGE OUTFALL.

——:oo:——

THE magnificent works of the Southern Outfall at Crossness Point are three miles below Woolwich. The spot may be reached by the new road which the Metropolitan Board have made direct from Plumstead station across the marsh to Crossness, in which case a splendid panorama of hill will be opened on the spectators right hand; or we may take a trip on the river. The Works, from their magnitude and comprehensiveness, are unparalleled. Engines and reservoirs being on the same spot, what can be seen on the north side only in separate sections miles apart, can be all viewed at one and the same time at Crossness, and will repay any visitor the trouble of journeying so far; in fact, few foreigners of note who visit this country leave without inspecting the works.

The Crossness Works were constructed for the purpose of pumping up the sewage of South London, including all the parishes between Crossness (which is 14 miles below London Bridge) and Putney (which is 7 miles above London Bridge), in its course receiving the whole of the drainage of that immense area, computed to be 69 square miles, or 44,000 square acres, extending inland from the river to Croydon. This area contains a population of 1,100,000, or about one-third of the whole metropolis. The size of the main sewer at its upper end, next Richmond, is 4 feet diameter, and at Crossness it is 11 feet 6 inches diameter, which size it is through the whole of the town of Woolwich, and as far as the Deptford pumping station. Some notion may be obtained of the immense size of this sewer—the largest of modern main drainage works—when we mention that a heavy dragoon, fully mounted, could ride easily inside it for its entire length of 7½ miles. It brings down to Crossness an average of over 85,000,000 gallons daily throughout the year. It may be remarked that the three Water Companies who supply the South side of London deliver an average of 43,000,000 gallons. Some idea may be obtained of the enormous quantity of sewage that comes down to Crossness when it is recorded that the daily average supply varies from 66 millions of gallons in a dry weather month to 93 millions of gallons in a wet month. In consequence of the increased quantity coming down to Crossness, principally arising from the great spread of London out into the country, it has become necessary to augment the pumping power here by the addition of two large pumping engines of the locomotive type, working four very large centrifugal pumps, capable together of lifting 75 millions of gallons daily into the reservoirs.

A portion of the sewage brought to Crossness has been previously pumped and lifted 18 feet from the low level sewer into the outfall sewer at Deptford pumping station, which is a half-way pumping establishment for lifting the sewage from the low-lying districts. The high level sewer brings the sewage of the districts standing on high ground, such as Norwood, Clapham,

K

Tooting, &c.; the Effra branch brings the drainage of the Crystal Palace neighbourhood; and the low level sewer that of the low districts bordering on the banks of the Thames. The main sewage combined runs down to Crossness, taking up in its course the drainage of Greenwich, Eltham, Lewisham, Charlton, Woolwich, and Plumstead; and, arriving at Crossness, the whole is pumped from a depth of 21 feet below the marsh into a large brick covered-in reservoir, whose inside area is $6\frac{1}{2}$ acres, capable of containing about half a day's dry weather supply of sewage, or 24,000,000 gallons. The pumping goes on at Crossness night and day throughout the year—one gang of men relieving the other. The sewage is merely lifted into the reservoir to accumulate and abide the turn of the tide in the river, as directly the top of the flood tide has been reached the pentstock gates of the reservoir are opened into the river. The time necessary for emptying the reservoir by gravitation into the river is about two hours 40 minutes; the condition of the tide at the time of shutting off the reservoir from the river is about half ebb. In round numbers the sewage is discharged into the river 5 hours 20 min. out of the 24 hours of the day, and then at such a time that it does the least harm, and has little prospect of getting back to Woolwich or London. The town of Woolwich is $4\frac{1}{2}$ miles above Crossness, and the last particle of sewage is shut off from discharge into the river at about four hours before the turn of the tide; therefore, taking the velocity of the Thames at three miles an hour, it shows that the last of the sewage had arrived at a point $16\frac{1}{2}$ miles below Woolwich, in the meantime having been diluted and amalgamated with an immense bulk of brackish water. The Thames at Crossness is about 2,400 feet in width, and has a sectional area at mean spring tides high water of over 75,000 superficial feet, so, on the whole, it must be confessed that the point of discharge of the London sewage at the south side of the river at Crossness was a judiciously and well conceived plan of the Engineer of the Metropolitan Board of Works, Sir Joseph Bazalgette.

The engines employed are very large, and are six in number, four of the rotary beam type, each 125 nominal horse-power, and two of the locomotive type, each 250 nominal horse-power, or 1,000 horse power in all. They are worked up to double this power, and during the time they have been in work have given entire satisfaction. There are 19 boilers, 17 to work the four beam engines and two to work the deep well engines.

The whole appearance of the Crossness establishment is both pleasing and unique, forming as it does a complete and isolated colony, making its own gas, and obtaining its water from two deep wells—one now noted to all geologists as having been the means of settling a theory that coal existed beneath London. This boring went 1,065 feet below the surface, passing through the tertiary; the chalk 631 feet, the upper green sand 65 feet, the Gault clay 175 feet, no lower green sand, but into hard red Devoneau rods, the mass of some 5,000 feet of rocks being absent in this neighbourhood. The dwellings, of which there are 23, can hardly be surpassed in their sanitary arrangements and architectural appearance. The cost of this outfall and the outfall sewers connected with it was about three-quarters of a million pounds; and to show that the Metropolis gets a return for its expenditure, we may mention that the mortality in 1879 averaged only 23·3 per thousand, which is lower than any of the other capitals in Europe. In the years 1666 to 1673, the mortality of London was 80 per thousand, showing a great improvement in modern times.

The works were opened by the Prince of Wales and the Duke of Edinburgh on April 4th, 1865.

It may not be out of place to mention that the main drainage outlet for the whole of the main drainage of the northern section of the Metropolis, is in the parish of Woolwich, that part of Woolwich lying on the Essex side of the river and extending down as far as the mouth of Barking Creek. It is there that the whole of the accumulated sewage of North London is poured out twice a day into the river, the same as is done at Crossness, adopting the same time of discharge; the north side outlet is two miles nearer London than the south side outlet at Crossness; the average quantity of sewage discharged daily at Barking is about 75,000,000 gallons; the reservoir there is in the same style as that at Crossness, but 9½ acres in area, and equal to a cubical contents of 36,000,000 gallons. There are three main sewers that join the reservoir, the High Level and Mid Level bringing down the sewage from the north and north-west of London by gravitation, and the Low Level only having come from the Abbey Mills Pumping Station by gravitaton, it having been pumped there from a much lower level (34 feet) and lifted into its outfall sewer. The size of these three sewers are 9 feet 6 inches by 9 feet 6 inches each, standing upon a high embankment running for miles across the Marsh. The population of the north side of the Metropolis, served by this outlet, is about $2\frac{1}{2}$ millions, or about double that of the south side.

The engines at Abbey Mills are worth mentioning. There are eight engines, each 142 nominal horse power, with double acting pumps attached; Abbey Mills Pumping Station is four miles from the outlet at Barking.

The whole of the Metropolitan Main Drainage Works were designed by Sir Joseph Bazalgette, and have cost about £5,000,000.

VIEW FROM THE RIVER AT ERITH.

GEOLOGY.

OR the following information on the Geology of the Woolwich district we are indebted to two able contributors. Mr. Wells says :—The chalk formation which rises into high cliffs at Dover extends to Woolwich, but is there found at a considerable depth from the surface of the land. In Charlton, where deep excavations have been made for ballast, the chalk is covered by 50 feet of sand. In Wickham Lane it rises nearer to the surface. This immense deposit of chalk may well fill the mind with astonishment when we remember that every particle of it was once endued with life, and formed a part of some organic being. Above the chalk, to the height of 450 feet, rises Shooters' Hill, an isolated mass of London clay. On the slopes of this hill, facing the river are terraces of gravel. Woolwich, Plumstead, and Bostol Commons are gravel terraces. Below these terraces there is usually a large deposit of yellow silicious sand. The summit of Shooters' Hill consists of a tolerably thick deposit of gravel. A great many of the stones composing this gravel are abraded flints, but the majority consist of pebbles of a coarse silicious character, abraded fragments of a rock which is not to be found in the county, if in the kingdom. The only way in which we can account for these deposits is by the glacial theory. Icebergs, we know, are formed on the precipitous coasts of Arctic or Antarctic countries. The glaciers of the mountains feed them for ages with ice, clay, and pebbles, till some storm rends them from the coast and launches them on the deep, whose currents convey them to warmer climes. Here they melt away, and deposit in the bed of the ocean the insoluble materials they contain. Those who have seen the majestic ice islands of the Southern Ocean, miles in extent and several hundreds of feet high, will readily understand the reasonableness of this theory. When under cultivation the land which is now the Raglan Road used to bear unmistakable traces of an ancient sea margin, the plough turning up a deposit of shell marl. Carbonised hazel trees and nuts have been found in the form of brown coal in deep excavations in the Dockyard and Plumstead Marshes, and the student may find, at low tide, on the north shore of the river at Dagenham, the stumps of numerous trees — the sole remains of an ancient forest, which once occupied the valley of the Thames. Some very large fossil oysters were found, a few years ago, in the Royal Arsenal and in Plumstead Road, while excavating for the new sewers. They are preserved in the Royal Carriage Department Pattern Room.

Mr. Freeman, of Plumstead, says :—At Charlton occurs one of the best exposures of the upper secondary formation, viz., the chalk, with its numerous and beautiful fossils, the Echinodermata shells, &c., to be seen around London. Capped by the Thanet sand and the commencement of the Eocene strata, the plastic clays known amongst geologists as the Woolwich beds, are rich in fossil remains, such as Melania, Cerethium, Cyrena, &c. Woolwich itself, being situated on the alluvium in the great Thames valley, is surrounded on the south and east by those immense gravel beds, " the old haven beds," which is an ancient raised sea beach, and forming the basement bed of that great isolated lump of London clay, Shooters' Hill, which is again topped by the glacial drift, and well seen by the roadside of Shrewsbury Lane, opposite Tower House ; and then towards Wickham, as seen in Dawson's brick pit, we make our first acquaintance in this locality of the Pleistocene drift—that charnel house of the great mammals, who roamed wild over the land before the British Channel existed.

The " Woolwich Beds" are remarkable for their ever changing structure. In Kent, however, there is none of the brightly coloured plastic clay that occurs so generally in the western part of the London basin. The Woolwich beds are about 50 or 60 feet thick, and consists of alternations of sand, beds of pebbles, and shell beds. The shell beds must have been deposited in a river, or estuary, for some of the shells are of a kind that could not have existed in salt water ; but there are oysters which show that the beds are not altogether fresh water. The fossils of these beds are most abundant in number, but not in kind, few species being found. Altogether, Woolwich locality is very interesting in its geological history. Bones of the rhinoceros, elephant, wild ox, and other animals, have been frequently found in the brick earth at Erith, and a valuable collection was formerly preserved in the Mechanics' Institution at Woolwich.

The Woolwich Infant School, Royal Arsenal.—May 20th, 1874.

WOOLWICH CHRONOLOGY.

Shewing the Dates of Remarkable Events in the History of Woolwich and its neighbourhood.

A.D.
457—Battle of Crayford—Hengist, King of Kent, slew 4,000 men, and survivors fled towards London.
670 – Barking Monastery founded. This house, which became very rich and great must have had an influence on the early growth of Woolwich (B. Wells).
1086 — Woolwich described as " Hulviz" in Domesday Book.
1178—Lesness Abbey founded.
1236—Inundation of marshes near Woolwich. Many inhabitants perished, and herds of cattle.
1279—Abbot of Lesness Abbey recovered the "Great Marsh" at Plumstead. Fourteen years after he enclosed the "Smaller Marsh."
1397—Date of the oldest tomb in old Woolwich Church, recorded in "Weever's Funeral Monuments."
1480—The "Great Harry" launched about this year; supposed to have been built at Woolwich.
1514—The "Harry Grace de Dieu" built at Woolwich Dockyard.

A.D.
1520—Lesness Abbey suppressed.
— About this year, in middle of Henry the Eighth's reign, the pippin was brought "from over the sea" and established at Plumstead. (Phillips.)
1527—2,000 acres of Plumstead Marsh inundated.
1539—Barking Monastery suppressed.
1545—Goldsmith's Almshouses established.
1563 - Jacob Ancontius, an Italian, recovered 600 acres of Marshes, and by various hands 1,000 more were restored soon after, leaving the remainder under water for many years.
1540—Woolwich Dockyd. enlarged.
1667—Prince Rupert fortified the Royal Arsenal.
1668—Earliest mention of Royal Carriage Department, Woolwich.
1695—Earliest mention of Royal Laboratory, Woolwich.
1701—Date of the oldest map of Royal Arsenal extant.
1716—Explosion at Moorfields, and

the Gun Foundry removed to Woolwich.

1716—Sept. 20. Andrew Schalch appointed master founder at Woolwich.

1719—Gun Foundry completed.

1739—Woolwich Church rebuilt.

1757—Riot in Woolwich Dockyard.

1775—First half of R.A. Barracks built.

1776—Andrew Schalch died.

1780—Ordnance Hospital (A.S.C. Barracks) partly built.

1797—Mutiny of Royal Artillery.

1801—Rl. Military Academy built.

1802—Fire in Arsenal; destroyed many models.

— Western half of R.A. Barracks added.

1804—The wall of the Rl. Arsenal raised in height throughout. It was originally about 8 ft. high.

1805—The Warren first called "The Royal Arsenal."

1806—Cambridge (Royal Marine) Barracks built.

— Ordnance Hospital enlarged.

1807—Woolwich Board of Commissioners established.

1809—Russell and Webb gibbeted at Shooters' Hill for highway robby.

1814—Allied Sovereigns visited Woolwich.

1820—Rotunda opened.

— March. Mr. Parker and his female servant murdered in Mulgrave Place, Woolwich, and their house robbed and fired by James Nesbitt, a tailor, afterwards executed at Maidstone.

1822—The Tally-ho, Woolwich "opposition" coach, upset on Blackheath Hill with 15 passengers, all of whom were injured, some fatally.

1824—The first steam machinery erected in the Royal Arsenal by the elder Brunel.

1831—Feb. 6. Four lads drowned in Bowater Pond, while scrambling on the ice.

1832—May 3. Mr. C. J. Carttar elected coroner at the age of 21, in succession to his father, who held the office 21 years.

— May 10. Woolwich Equitable Gas Company founded.

1833—Woolwich Ropeyd abolish'd.

— Nov. George Bodle, farmer, of Plumstead, aged 81, and 20 years churchwarden, poisoned. His grandson, John Bodle, was arrested, tried at Maidstone, and acquitted. He was received with great rejoicing at Plumstead, but he afterwards confessed the crime while a convict.

1834—March 17. Woolwich Steam Packet Company originated. Capital £5,000 in £5 shares.

— First omnibuses run from Woolwich to London by Shillibeer and Wheatley.

1835—May. Elizabeth Browning, landlady of the Britannia, Woolwich, murdered by Patrick Carroll, a corporal of Marines, who stabbed her with his bayonet at the tavern bar. He was executed.

1836—Feb. Inhabitants of Woolwich petitioned against the proposed railway. The bill was defeated, and the town was said to be "saved from destruction."

— Feb. A Marine named Saundry died after being flogged with 100 lashes. Great public excitement, but the jury found a verdict of "Died by the visitation of God."

— Aug. A young Turk, studying at the Academy, died, and was buried in the grounds of the Depot, New Road.

— Nov. Woolwich Bank failed: liabilities, £14,000; assets, £7,000.

— Dec. Star and Garter, Powis Street, burnt, and Dr. Allinson's house, next door, partly destroyed.

1837—April 21. Rev. Hugh Frazer.

many years rector of Woolwich, died, and was succeeded by Rev. W. Greenlaw, of Northolt, Midx.

1837—May. Four convicts escaped from the Dockyard and were re-captured in Shooters' Hill Wood, which the troops surrounded. Such escapes were frequent.

1838—July 5. Feast in honour of the Queen's Coronation to 4,500 artillerymen and their families on the Barrack Field. Grand review same day by Marshal Soult.

— Woolwich Literary Institution formed.

1839 - Feb. Woolwich Workhouse abolished.

— March. Charlotte Rees, aged 17, accidentally shot by James Wooley, at Tappy's Place, Powis Street. He was practising with a carbine at a butcher's block, when the ball passed through the wooden cottage wall and penetrated her head.

— March. Convict hulk Gany-mede upset at Woolwich Dock-yard in the night. No lives lost. The Warrior hulk replaced her.

— May 26. Sergt.-Major William Shepherd, R.A., shot on parade in front of the barracks by Geo. Willis, a young artilleryman, on a Sunday morning. The de-ceased was buried with great honour, Lord Bloomfield, Com-mandant, following. The mur-derer was hanged at Maidstone, on July 4.

— May. A cadet, son of Colonel Bull, killed by a ball fired during mortar practice on Woolwich Common, as he lay unobserved on the grass.

— July. Esplanade 300 feet long, bowling green, and tea gardens, established at North Woolwich, by the proprietor of the Old Barge House.

1839—Nov. Insubordination at Royal Military Academy; 14 cadets dismissed. Mr. Lewis Davis, pawnbroker, accused of assisting one to desert, but ex-culpated.

1840 — Jan. The "New Police" introduced into Woolwich.

— April 22. Sir Alexander Dick-son, Director General, R.A., died. Buried at Plumstead with grand ceremony.

— Oct. Mr. Jeremy, first stipen-diary magistrate at Woolwich, opened the Police Court at William Street, which the in-inhabitants had just built for a Town Hall, but sold to the Com-missioners of Police for £1,525, afterwards building another hall close by. Mr. Grove was Mr. Jeremy's colleague.

— Oct. 18. Riot of cadets at Charlton Fair. About 50 cadets, masked and carrying bludgeons, cleared the fair and did much damage.

— Dec. 25. Great fire on Woolwich Common. Five houses just built, next the Barrack Tavern, were destroyed.

— Dec. Robert Greenlaw, son of the Rector, accidentally shot while out shooting behind the Academy. Another son was afterwards killed by a similar accident in India.

1841—April. Waterman Steam Packet Company commenced running.

— May 31. Canton taken.

— June 14. Homicide in R.A. Barracks. Bombardier John Grice shot by Gunner James McGarity. Through absence of motive, and the accused being drunk, he was convicted of man-slaughter and imprisoned for one year.

—June 21. Launch of the Tra-falgar at Woolwich by the Queen and Prince Albert.

1842—Nov. Woolwich Dockyard enlarged for steam factory, graving docks, &c.

1844—March 26. Consumers' Gas Company formed.

— May. St. Thomas's district formed.

— May 18. Parochial Almshouses established.

1845—Sept. 17. Explosion in Royal Laboratory. John Crake (master rocket maker), Henry Butters, sen., Henry Butters, jun., Robert Burbage, Michael Purtell, Samuel Hendley, and Alexander Leonard, killed while breaking up unserviceable fuzes.

— Nov. 8. Fall of part of St. John's Church while building.

1845-6—The Sikh War.

1846—July 2. Visit of Ibrahim Pacha to Woolwich.

— Aug. 15. Death of Lord Bloomfield, formerly commandant.

— North Woolwich Railway laid.

1847—Mar. 23. St. John's Church consecrated.

— May 15. Dockyard Brigade formed at Woolwich. 960 men attested.

1848—May 8. Tom Cribb died at Woolwich. Spring and other pugilists attended the funeral, and the Earl of Glasgow gave £10 towards the monument in the churchyard.

1849—April 17. Woolwich County Court established.

— July 21. North Kent Railway opened to Woolwich

1850—June 18. Woolwich Baths opened.

—Dec. 22. Rev. W. Greenlaw died.

1851—Jan. Rev. H. Brown (incumbent of Boreham, Essex) appointed Rector of Woolwich.

—June. North Woolwich Gardens established.

—July 18. Alderman Salomons on his first election refused to make oath "on the true faith of a Christian." The words afterwards omitted from the oath.

1851—Aug. 21. 1,555 Woolwich children taken to the Great Exhibition by Mr. J Charlton.

1852 - May 22. Launch of Agamemnon.

— Aug. 18. First election of Woolwich Local Board of Health, 126 candidates.

—Nov. 1. Mr J. Pitt Taylor appointed Judge of Woolwich and Greenwich County Courts.

— Dec. 27. Nos. 12, 13, 14, and 15, High Street burnt.

1853—April. Rev. W. Acworth, of Rothley, appointed Vicar of Plumstead, on resignation of Rev. H. J. Shackleton.

—June. Woolwich drainage commenced.

1854—Feb. to April. Departure of troops from Woolwich to the Crimea.

—May 13. Launch of the Royal Albert, 121 guns, by the Queen.

—July 31. Opening of Plumstead Water Works.

— Sept. 20. Battle of the Alma.

— Nov. 5. Battle of Inkermann.

1855 - Jan. 17. Poll concerning Woolwich Cemetery. For, 848; against, 502.

— H.M.S. Perseverance capsized in the Dockard.

— April 29. St. James's Church, Plumstead, opened.

— Sept. 12. Firework display at inner range on fall of Sebastopol.

— Dec. 3. Explosion in East Laboratory. John Kirwin, Wm. Wallace, Henry S. Langham, and Thomas Holland killed while making Hale's rockets.

1856—Jan. 3. Woolwich Cemetery opened. Consecration by Bishop of Oxford. Woolwich churchyard closed.

— Jan. 10. Removal of Sappers and Miners (Royal Engineers) from Woolwich to Chatham.

1856—Feb. 1. First meeting of Plumstead District Board of Works.

— Mar. 13. Royal Arsenal T Pier opened. One thousand of the siege train R.A., landed from the Crimea, and were inspected by the Queen on Barrack Field.

— May 6. Explosion in rocket shed. William Powell mortally wounded, and 11 others injured.

— May 17. Another explosion in Arsenal. Wm. Flack, foreman of percussion cap composition shed, a man named Taylor, and a boy named Flack, were killed.

— May 29. Peace rejoicings at close of Russian war

— July 3. Public reception of Sir W. Fenwick Williams, of Kars, appointed commandant at Woolwich.

— Oct. 23. The last convicts removed from Woolwich.

1857—March 10. Garrison order issued permitting soldiers to wear moustaches.

— April 23. Murder of Corporal Long, R.M., on board the Hebe, at Woolwich, by Geo. Bave, a seaman, who stabbed him with a bayonet, and was hanged at Maidstone.

— May 10. Indian Mutiny begun.

— May and June. Great reduction at the Arsenal. 1050 persons sent to the colonies, £6000 being subscribed for the purpose.

— June 18. Hulk "Defence" destroyed by fire at the Arsenal.

— Nov. 21. Great concert in Carriage Square for sufferers in Indian Mutiny.

1858—April. Walpole Road made.

— May 31. Mr. Francis Pellatt, principal storekeeper, killed by being thrown from his carriage in Plumstead Road. Public funeral at Plumstead on June 5.

— Oct. 6. Attempted murder of Police Inspector Budd. Shot near the Dockyard by Edward Mark Councill, who was sentenced to death, but transported for life.

1858—Oct. 23. Launch of the Edgar, 91 guns.

1859—Jan. 5. Church rates defeated at Woolwich by a poll. For, 591 ; against, 702.

— Marine Infirmary (Red Barracks) built.

— April 25. St Margaret's, Plumstead, consecrated.

— July 16. Plumstead station opened.

— July 27. First meeting at Woolwich to establish Volunteer Corps.

— Nov. 11. Early Closing Riot.

1860 – War with China.

— July. Eleanor Road made.

— Aug. 29. Consecration of new ground added to Plumstead churchyard

1861 – Jan. 3. Old Arsenal bell cracked, after doing duty at the gates since 1699.

— March 15. Plumstead Water Works bought by Mr. L. Davis for £20,400, and sold by him within a month to the Kent Company.

— April 1. Military Police established at Woolwich.

— April 20. Steam Flour Mills burnt.

— July 8. Murder of Sergeant Murphy, R.A., in the Arsenal guardroom, by Gunner Peter Masterson; hanged at Maidstone Sept. 19.

— Oct. 11. Mr. Joseph Grisbrook, of Woolwich, accidently shot himself at Tenterden.

— Nov. 20. Testimonial to Mr. R. Ruegg, as promoter of Woolwich improvements

— Dec. Threatened outbreak with America over "The Trent affair" during the Civil War.

1862—March 27. First Royal Artillery Steeple Chases. Challenge Cup established.

1862— July 15. French Gardes Band entertained at Woolwich by R.A. Band.

— July 16. Fête on Viceroy of Egypt's Yacht at Arsenal.

— Oct. and Nov. Great reductions in the Arsenal. 5000 discharged.

1863—Feb. 12. Sir W. Armstrong, Superintendent Royal Gun Factories, resigned.

— March. £7,000 voted to pave Woolwich.

— March 10. Prince of Wales's marriage. Great festivities at Woolwich, and fireworks on Barrack Field.

— May 14. Sensation caused by suicide of Mr. Roberts, baker, Coleman Street. Verdict "Temporary Insanity." Frances Paxton, his servant, who accused him of inciting her to poison his wife, was herself sentenced to three years' imprisonment.

— Aug. 11. The Queen embarked at Woolwich. Workmen in Arsenal were forbidden to look out of the windows under pain of dismissal, an order which was much ridiculed.

— Oct. 3. Two Arsenal foremen charged with stealing stores. One sentenced to 3 years' and the other to twelve months' imprisonment.

— Nov. 2. Consecration of St. George's Garrison church. Building cost £16,000.

1864 – April 6. Colonel Bingham, Dep.-Adjutant-General at Woolwich, died. Buried at Plumstead with military honours, April 12, Duke of Cambridge attending.

— April 13. Garibaldi's visit to Woolwich.

— April 30. Henry Maudslay buried at Woolwich.

— May. Rev. Jas. Adair McAllister succeeded Rev: W. Ackworth as Vicar of Plumstead.

1864— May 31. Gen. Warde succeeded Sir Richard Dacres as commandant.

— June 11. Death of Mr. W. Nokes, Clerk to the Magistrates.

— June 14. Suicide of Mr. W. Sloman.

— July 22. First County Review at Woolwich.

— Oct. 1. The Erith explosion, Saturday morning, at quarter to seven. Two magazines and two powder barges blew up. Geo. Rayner, John Hubbard, John Eaves, and eight others killed; several injured, and great damage to property for miles round.

— Dec. 16. Collision in Blackheath Tunnel. Seven killed and many injured.

1865—April 4. Crossness Outfall opened by the Prince of Wales.

— Dec. 15. Victoria Ale Stores, North Woolwich, burnt. Damage £250,000.

1866—March 3. Strike in building trades at Woolwich for short time. Saturday half-holiday established March 20, and strike ended.

— Herbert Hospital built.

— March 25. Lieut. Gorges, R.A., thrown from his horse on Woolwich Common and killed.

— Sept. 25. Death of Mr. H. Bland, Clerk to the Burial Board, &c.

— Oct. 1. Gun cotton magazine at Arsenal exploded. No one hurt.

— Dec. 15. Inquest on Mr. Eugene Murray, found in the Thames after being missed since Nov. 10.

1867—March 19. Consecration of St. Paul's, Charlton.

— July 16. Visit of the Sultan of Turkey.

— Sept. 6. Collision between the Metis and the Wentworth; four lives lost.

— Sept. 29. Abyssinian expedition started.

— Oct. 5. Explosion in East Laboratory at 11 a.m. on Saturday; 24 cartridge boys burnt, six of whom died soon after.

1867—Dec. Fenian fever ; 7,000 special constables sworn in at Woolwich, Plumstead, and Charlton.

1868—April 13. Storming of Magdala.

— Jan. 13. Mr. Traill, magistrate, resigned, and was succeeded by Mr. Patteson.

— March 10. Woolwich Union formed. First meeting of Guardians, April 15.

— May 16. Closing of Woolwich and Plumstead Savings' Bank, established 1816.

— June. Plumstead added to the Borough.

— June 13. Return of Colonel Milward from Abyssinia.

— June 19. Prince Arthur left Royal Military Academy.

— Dec. Clothing Store removed to Pimlico. Great reductions in Dockyard and Arsenal. Relief Fund, about £3,000 raised, and 1,800 persons sent to Canada.

1869—April 1. Woolwich Division Royal Marines abolished.

— April 17. Supression of the " Deptford Spec."

— May 5. Sir Thos. M. Wilson died at Charlton.

— July 1. Sir David Wood succeeded Sir E. Warde, as Commandant.

— July 13. The last ship (Thalia) launched at Woolwich Dockyard.

— Aug. 1. Prince Arthur, after serving in Engineers and Artillery, went to Canada and joined Rifle Brigade, with which he returned to Woolwich in following year.

— Sept. 18. Woolwich Dockyard closed.

1870—Feb. 2.—Two promoters of " Dept. Spec." fined £100 each.

1870—Feb. 9. Col. Milward succeeded Col. Boxer as Superintendent of Royal Laboratory.

— Feb. 14. Army Service Corps formed.

— March 4. Mutiny at Military Train Barracks. Corps disbanded March 16, and prisoners released.

— March 10. Greenwich agreed to pay Woolwich £10,000 for share of Workhouse.

— April 2. Laying Foundation Stone of Workhouse, Plumstead.

— April 3. Death of Dr. A. W. Allinson, aged 37 years.

— April 4. Fire at Nelson Inn.

— April 15. Disbandment of Dockyard Volunteers.

— April 25. Injunction to protect Plumstead Common rights.

— May 16. Five men suffocated in a well at Beckton.

— May 30. 190 emigrants went from Woolwich to Canada, and 304 on June 11.

— June. Fenian scare at Woolwich.

— June 13. 94th Regiment left Woolwich.

— June 15. Mr. Lloyd elected Metropolitan Board member for Plumstead District.

— July 2 County Review at Woolwich.

— July 9. Attempt to restore Woolwich Market.

— July 15. Outbreak of Franco-German War.

— July 26. 1st Batt. Rifle Brigade and Prince Arthur at Woolwich.

— Sept. 6. H.M.S. Captain foundered.

— Sept. 8. Chichester boat accident. Rev. C. Hind and five boys drowned off Royal Arsenal.

— Nov. 29. First election of London School Board.

1871—Depot Barracks built.

— Jan. Woolwich Dockyard transferred to War Office.

1871—Jan. 13. Proof of 35-ton gun, "Woolwich Infant."

— Jan. 29. Capitulation of Paris.

— Feb. Narrow tramway commenced in Arsenal.

— April 4 to 13. Murphy riots at Woolwich.

— July. Woolwich busy owing to outbreak of Franco-Prussian war

— April 25. The Eltham murder. Jane Maria Clousen, a young woman, brutally murdered in Kidbrook Lane. She lingered insensible until April 30. Edmund Walter Pook, 20, a printer at Greenwich, apprehended May 1st, and after an exciting trial, was acquitted at Old Bailey, July 15.

— May 4. Prince Arthur presented with address by the Local Board on his majority.

— May 20. Commandant's office, R.A. Barracks, burnt.

— Aug. 2. Decision in favour of public rights on Plumstead Common.

— Aug. 3. Workhouse at Plumstead opened.

— Aug. 16. Hidden well excitement. Mrs. Balchin suffocated in a buried pool at 45, King Street, and several similar pitfalls discovered.

— Nov. 29. First School Board election.

1872—March. Charlton Fair abolished by Order in Council.

— March 28. Girls' factory in Arsenal closed.

— April 16. Three children named Pearson burnt to death at 14, Plumstead Road.

— April. "Gunfire" established at Woolwich.

— Oct. 15. "Turn out" in Arsenal shell foundry against "condemned work." Satisfactorily adjusted.

— Oct. 23. Death of Mr. George Hall Graham.

1872—Nov. 4. Reduction of the hours in Arsenal to 54 per week.

— Nov. 18. Louis Buonaparte (Prince Imperial) joined Royal Military Academy.

—Dec. 2. Strike of gas stokers at Beckton.

—Dec. 26. Death of Mr. J. Richardson, Sanitary Inspector, Plumstead.

1873—Jan. 9. Emperor Napoleon III. died at Chislehurst, aged 64. Laid in State Jan. 14. Buried Jan. 15.

— Feb. 1. Great fire at Royal Military Academy.

—June 16. Meeting of the Prince and Princess of Wales with the Cesarewith and Cesarevna of Russia, at the Royal Arsenal.

—June 21. Visit of Shah of Persia to Woolwich. Grand proceedings.

—July 18. Alderman Sir D. Salomons, M.P., died, aged 76.

— Aug. Anglesea Hill lowered.

— Oct. 16. Death of Mr. Traill.

— Oct. 25. Dreadful boat accident. Nine persons—Geo. Gray, Thos. Smith, Patrick Martin, Henry Tanner, Joseph Joscelyn, Samel Jones, William Piper, Patrick Lanna, and John Taylor, drowned by the upsetting of a small boat while attempting to cross the river to their work at North Woolwich in a dense fog, at half-past five Saturday morning. £777 was subscribed for their families. Digby (waterman) and John Wright were saved.

— Nov. and Dec. Preparations for Ashantee War.

1874—Jan. 24. Torpedo exploded in Arsenal, killing Herbert Edward Baker, and wounding Fishenden, M'Coan, and Dymott.

— Feb. 1. Mr. Gladstone's speech in Beresford Square.

— Feb. 4. Capture of Coomassie.

1874—March 20. Return of Royal Artillery from Ashantee. High tide, which did great damage.

— March 27. Death of Mr. Maude, magistrate. Succeeded by Mr. Balguy.

— May 20. Visit of Czar of Russia. Great day at Woolwich.

— June 30. 93rd Highlanders stationed at Woolwich.

— July 4. General D'Aguilar succeeded Sir David Wood as commandant

— Sept. 19. Death of Mr. John Pettman, inventor of the Pettman fuze. Public funeral.

— Oct. 2. Regent's Park Explosion.

— Nov. 17. The Cospatrick burnt at sea.

— Nov. 29. Wreck of the La Plata, Mr. Henley's telegraph ship, in the Bay of Biscay. 58 persons, chiefly from Woolwich, were drowned, and 17 saved.

— Dec. 31. Death of Col. Milward, R.A., Superintendent Royal Laboratory, aged 49. Public funeral at Charlton Cemetery, Jan. 5.

1874-5 (Winter). Outbreak of diptheria at Soldiers' Huts on Woolwich Common.

1875—Jan. 12. Opening of first new Board School at Plumstead (Burrage Grove).

— Feb. 16. Prince Imperial (Louis Napoleon) of France passed out of Royal Military Academy.

— March 1. Colonel Fraser, R.A., assumed superintendence of the Royal Laboratory.

— March 9. Death of Mr. John Graydon, chief dispenser, Royal Arsenal. Buried March 13th.

— March 17. Mr. W. Farnfield elected clerk of the Plumstead District Board, on resignation of Mr. Dale. For Farnfield, 19; Hughes, 17.

— April 6. Re-assessment of Government property made.

Woolwich increased from the sum of £34,840 to £40,450; Plumstead, from £12,745 to £20,743; Charlton, from £1,322 to £1,600; Kidbrook, from £33 to £2,000.

1875—April 12. Woolwich Postal District established.

— April. Colonel Middleton, R.A., died en route to Lisbon.

— April 23. Captain Hardinge Browne, R.A., killed on the railway at Esher.

— May 2. The Rev. Canon Brown, Rector of Woolwich, died in his robes at the parish church, on Sunday morning, aged 70. He was buried with great respect on May 7th.

— May 21. Opening of Earl Street (Plumstead) Board Schools

— May 24. Explosion of gun cotton shell in Cap Factory, Royal Arsenal; Charles Young, foreman, and Joseph Walstow, his assistant, killed. Both buried in Plumstead churchyard, May 29.

— May 29. Commission of enquiry as to Bostal Heath.

— June 6. Mutinous destruction of harness at Royal Artillery Barracks

—June 13. Fire at Pier Music Hall.

— June 25. Consecration of the United Military Lodge of Freemasons at Plumstead.

— June 25. Death of Mr. W. G. Hudson, Burrage Estate.

— July 1. Embarkation of Duke and Duchess of Edinburgh at Royal Arsenal, for Russia.

— July 14. First edition of this book was published.

— July 15. Foundation stone of St. Michael and All Angel's Church, Woolwich, by the Bishop of Rochester.

— July 17. Death of Mr. J. A. Rastrick, Woolwich Common; aged 60.

— July 21. 93rd Highlanders left

Woolwich for Shorncliffe. 77th Regiment stationed at Woolwich.

1875— July 22. New Rolling Mills, Royal Gun Factories, opened.

— July 26. Woolwich Steam Packet Company transferred to London Steamboat Company by resolution ratified Aug. 12.

— Aug. 1. Gen. Younghusband R.A., appointed Superintendent Royal Gun Factories, vice Gen. F. A. Campbell, C.B., appointed Director of Artillery.

— July 28. Roads on Woolwich Common and Barrack Field surrendered to local authorities

— Aug. 9. Death of Mr. George Starling.

— Aug. 24. Rev. Hon. A. Anson (vicar of Sedgley) appointed Rector Woolwich. Inducted Oct. 24.

— Sept. 6. Mr. Wm. Angus, assistant manager, Royal Laboratory, killed accidentally at Canterbury Railway Station ; aged 50 years Succeeded by Mr. R. Low.

— Sept. 14 Last company of Royal Engineers left Woolwich

— Sept. 17. First proof of 81 ton gun.

— Sept 26. The Rev. A. Robertson left St James's Church, Plumstead, for St. Saviour's, Brixton. Since deceased.

— Oct. 20. Presentation from Local Board and townspeople to Quartermaster W. Richie, R.A., on removal to Colchester.

— Nov. 4. Death of Mr. Joseph Whomes, jun., organist, aged 26.

— Nov. 15. Disastrous flood, caused by overflow of Thames at Woolwich, Charlton, &c.

— Nov. 24. Proposal of the Rector to rebuild Woolwich Church.

— Nov. 25 Decision against Peculiar People : an elder sentenced to 4 days' Imprisonment for refusing medical aid to a child.

— Dec. 22. Burning of the Goliath, training ship, at Grays A schoolmaster and about 18 boys lost.

1875—Christmas Day. Choir introduced at Woolwich Church.

— Dec. 26. Fatal fire at 35, High Street. Bridget O'Brien, servant, burnt to death.

1876—Jan. 3. Destruction by fire of the training ship Warspite, near Charlton Pier. No lives lost.

— Jan. 8. Death of Mr. N. Norman, amateur florist.

— Jan. Engineers' strike at Erith.

— Jan. 22. Collapse of the " Co-operative Bank."

— Feb. 1. Soldiers' Home, Hill Street, Woolwich, opened.

— Feb. 17. Fall of a house in Salutation Alley, Woolwich ; Mrs. Bridget Hayes killed.

— Feb. 21. Public Library meeting at Woolwich ; uproarious rejection of the scheme.

— Feb. 22. Burglary at Charlton House.

— Feb. 28. Burglary at Lord Teynham's, Shooters' Hill.

— April 29. Shooting match— 77th Reg. v. 26th Kent R.V. ; score : 77th Reg., 996 ; 26th Kent, 982.

— May 4. Presentation of colours to the 77th Reg. by the Duke of Cambridge. Reg. left Woolwich May 25th, and succeeded by 5th Fusileers.

— May 6. First demonstration on Plumstead Common.

— May 11. Death of Sir John Maryon Wilson, aged 74. Buried on 17th at Charlton Cemetery.

— June 17. Graydon memorial unveiled at Woolwich Cemetery.

— June 27. Election of Mr. H. O. Thomas, surveyor of Woolwich, in place of Mr. J. Barnett, superannuated.

— July 1, 2, 3. Riotous proceedings at Plumstead Common. Mr. J. De Morgan and others summoned at Police Court on July 7th. Committed for trial Aug. 5th.

— July. Royal Arsenal Association of Foremen instituted

1876—Aug. 27. George Robinson, Wm. Foster, and Thos. Massey, of Woolwich, drowned near Crossness, by the upsetting of a sailing skiff.

— Sept. 9. Mr. Gladstone's speech at Blackheath, on "Bulgarian Atrocities."

— Sept. 21. A Woolwich "elder" of the Peculiar People sentenced to three months' imprisonment.

— Oct. 3. Death of Mr. W. T. Hearn, Woolwich.

— Oct. 19. Independencia, Brazilian ironclad, floated out of Woolwich Dockyard, after repairs.

— Oct. 20, 21. Trial at Maidstone of De Morgan and ten others for Plumstead Common riots. De Morgan sentenced to a month's imprisonment; another man fined £5; remainder acquitted. Tumultuous demonstration at Woolwich, Oct. 21.

— Oct. 27. Death of Mr. John Harris, of Plumstead.

— Nov. Activity in Arsenal, consequent on Russo-Turkish complications.

— Nov. 4. Release of De Morgan.

— Nov. 5. Great demonstration and burning of effigies on Plumstead Common.

— Nov. 8. Opening of Bloomfield Road Board Schools.

— Nov. 10. Death of Mr. F. Sales, Woolwich.

— Nov. 21. Wedding of Captain C. G. Leggitt and Miss Lizzie Wilson, at Charlton.

— Nov. 23. Death of Mr. George Cay, of Plumstead.

— Dec. Last public oil lamp (opposite Park Guard) abolished at Woolwich.

— Dec. 2. Rev. Dr. Raitt appointed to Presbyterian Church, New Road, in succession to Rev. W. M. Thompson.

— Dec. 26. Renewed disturbances at Plumstead Common : scene at the sand-pits.

1877—Jan. Marine Society boys transferred from temporary ship Clio to Conqueror, the new Warspite.

— Jan. 2. Another flood. Trinity Marsh and North Woolwich Gardens under water.

— Jan. 4. Resignation of Mr. H. Corkey, Workhouse Master.

— Jan. 10. Thos. Wm. Christian sentenced to 8 years' penal servitude for attempting to poison his landlady, Mrs. Bayley, at Kingston Terrace, Charlton

— Jan. 19. Sudden death of the Rev. A. De La Mare, Rector of St. Thomas's, while at a meeting of the Board of Guardians; aged 71.

— Jan. 26. The first Plumstead "Town Dinner."

— Jan. 27. Death of Mr. F. Johnson, aged 75.

— Feb. 6. Death of Mr. John Webber, aged 71.

— Feb. 8. Death of Mr. James Colquhoun, solicitor, aged 74.

— Feb. 18. (Sunday) Explosion of a 9-pr. shell at Depot Barracks

— March. Reorganization of Royal Artillery, and abolition of Depot Brigade.

— March. Rev. J. Teall left Queen Street Chapel, for Salem Chapel, Soho, after 16 years' ministry.

— March 18. Mrs. McFetridge died at Brewer Street, Woolwich, aged 100 years and 9 months

— April 29. Rev. A. Morris, appointed Rector of St. Thomas's.

— May. Increased activity in Government works consequent on Russo-Turkish War.

— May 7. Suicide of Mr. J. H. Herapath, relieving officer.

— May 10. Death of Mr. F. Pattison, Burrage Estate.

— May 23. Rifle Brigade, 3rd Batt., arrived at Woolwich, from

Shorncliffe. 5th Fusiliers, 2nd Batt., removed to Chatham.

1877—June 1. Shafts of New Forge in Gun Factories blown down.

— June 21. Visit of the Prince and Princess of Wales, Prince Albert Victor, and Prince George to the Warspite.

— June 26. Woolwich Local Board-room re-built.

— July. Helmets introduced for Royal Artillery, Infantry, &c.

— July. Army pensioners paid quarterly, in advance.

— July 4. Provincial meeting of Kentish Freemasons at Erith.

— July 12. Prince of Wales dined at R.A. Mess.

— July 20. Mr. Patteson, police magistrate resigned, and succeeded by Mr. J. Wyndham-Slade.

— July 22. Roads in Arsenal named and numbered.

— Aug. Prizes for skill at arms introduced into Royal Artillery.

— Aug. Increase of wages to foremen, Royal Arsenal.

— Oct. 18. Gas explosion at Elmhurst, Shooters' Hill (residence of Lord Ribblesdale, Rifle Brigade).

— Oct. 24. Dr. Baxter Langley sentenced to 18 months' imprisonment for fraud.

— Oct. 26. Metropolitan Board resolved to vote £16,000 to purchase Bostall Heath, Plumstead Common, and Shoulder of Mutton Green.

— Oct. 27. Captain Gillett, R.N., succeeded to Warspite, Captain Phipps having resigned.

— Oct. 27. Fire in spirit cellar of Melbourne Arms, Plumstead

— Nov. Salaries of principal foremen, Royal Arsenal, increased.

— Nov. 5. Second burning of effigies on Plumstead Common.

— Nov. 7. Rt. Hon. Gathorne Hardy, War Secretary, distributed prizes at Arsenal

1877—Nov. 15. Presentation to Rev. J. Teall.

— Nov. 16. Sudden death of Mr. R. T. Mew, of the London and County Bank, aged 43.

— Nov. 21. Dr. Webster, of Woolwich Union, elected to St. George's, Hanover Square, Infirmary: succeeded by Dr. Rice.

— Nov. 23 & 25, & Dec. 18. Presentations to Lieuts. Pownall and M'Caffery, R.A., on promotion.

— Dec. R.H.A. Band formed into Mounted Band, R.A.

— Dec. Thousands of young trees planted in the Royal Arsenal.

1878—Jan. 1. Rev. J. White left Trinity Church, Woolwich, appointed Principal of Cowley College, Oxford.

— Jan. 2. Inspr. Butt, of Shooters' Hill, appointed Superintendent of P Division.

— Jan. 9. Battery of Rl. Artillery and 90th Regiment sailed for the Cape (Zulu War).

— Jan. 15. Rev. C. Bull, Rector of St. John's, North Woolwich, in succession to Rev. W. F. Witts.

— Jan. 10. Mr. John Hewitt, historian, died at Lichfield, aged 71.

— Jan. 11. Frederick Craft, railway inspector, killed at Arsenal Station, while saving the life of a woman. Buried with much sympathy, Jan. 19th, and £500 was subscribed for his family.

— Jan. 15. New Greenwich Borough Liberal Association formed

— Jan. Bostall Heath taken over by the Metropolitan Board.

— Feb. Increased activity consequent on the "war vote of six millions," prior to Berlin Conference.

— Feb. Mr. Fred. Leslie's *debut* in London.

— Feb. 1. Opening of the Greenwich and Woolwich Railway.

— Feb. 4. Sale of Telegraph Works, North Woolwich.

— Feb. 15. New 12-pr. introduced.

— Feb. 17. Death of Rev. John

Cox, formerly of Queen Street Chapel, aged 89 years.

1878—Feb. 25, 26. Actions for libel: "Hughes v. Flanedy and Kimber."

— Feb. 26. Funeral of Mr. R. T. Lacey.

— March. End of Russo-Turkish war.

— March 4. Plumstead omnibus after running two years, stopped.

— March 8. Opening of Boys' Home, Beresford Street.

— March 9. Mr. Gladstone announced his retirement from Greenwich.

— March 9. Lead barge sunk at Arsenal; two men drowned.

— March 11. Death of Mr. Richard Rixon, aged 71 years.

— March 13. Fall of storehouses in Dockyard. 150 men in the ruins and many hurt; none fatally

— March 21. Mr. W. T. Jolly appointed Registrar of Marriages for Woolwich District; and the Rev. T. Tuffield, Registrar of Births for Arsenal District, both in succession to Mr. R. Rixon.

— April 18th. Floods at Slade Valley, Plumstead.

— April 21. Army Reserve called up. Great preparations in expectation of war with Russia.

— May 1. 3rd Batt., Rifle Brigade, at Woolwich, under Duke of Connaught

— June 11. Mr. E. Hughes elected solicitor of Woolwich Local Board; Mr. W Farnfield, resigned

— June 15th. Death of Mr. J. B. Bayly, aged 44.

— June, 18. Mark Mason's Lodge "Excelsior," opened at Plumstead.

— June 26. Mr. C. Marvin, Plumstead, arrested for divulging Foreign Office secrets; released next day, and finally acquitted.

— June 25. Mr. W. P. Jackson, Chairman, Woolwich Local Board, elected to Metropolitan Board, on retirement of Mr. G. Hudson.

1878—June 25. Funeral of Gen. McBean, 93rd Regt. Died at Woolwich; buried at Edinburgh.

— July 2. 3rd Batt., Rifle Brigade, left Woolwich for Aldershot.

— July 1. Consecration of St. Michael and All Angels' Church, Woolwich.

— July 4. Plumstead Commons Act passed.

— July 21. Launch of the Clacton-on-Sea Life Boat.

— July 22. Death of Mr. John Cowen, many years Chairman of Board of Guardians; aged 73. Funeral, July 27th.

— July 23. Presentation of 50 guineas and cup to Mr. C. Jolly, by the Freemasons.

— July 25. Murder at Crayford of his three children, by Richard Lewis Sands, beershop keeper, Greenwich, and suicide of the murderer.

— July 31. Consecration of St. James's, Plumstead; the Rev. J. Stilon Henning appointed perpetual curate.

— Aug. 18th Hussars at Woolwich.

— Aug. 7. Death of Mr. James Malings, aged 47. Funeral, Aug. 10.

— Aug. 7. Fire at Arsenal proof butts.

— Aug. 14. Death of Rev. W. Gill, formerly of Rectory Place Congregational Church, aged 65.

— Aug. 22. First experiment in military ballooning at Arsenal, by Captain Templer.

— Aug. 24. Death of Rev. F. S. Harrison at Charlton, aged 44.

— Aug. 27. Mr. J. Taylor elected chairman of Woolwich Local Board on retirement of Mr. W. P. Jackson, after presiding 14 years.

— Sept. 3 (Tuesday). Wreck of the Princess Alice, saloon steamer, just below Woolwich, by collision with the Bywell Castle, steam collier, about 8 p.m. There were about 750 persons on board, and about 600 perished ; the precise number was never ascertained. 530 were registered at Woolwich.

1878—Sept. 10. A young man named Barnes, on passage to Woolwich, fell into the engine-room of the steamboat Cupid, and was killed.

— Sept. 12. The first portion of the wreck removed.

— Sept. 13. Funeral of Mr. Fred. Whomes, organist, drowned in the Princess Alice, aged 32.

— Sept. 14. The Crusader balloon escaped from the Arsenal; recovered at Oxford the same day.

— Sept. 25. Princess Alice Concert at Woolwich Skating Rink.

— Oct. 25. Death of Police Constable Moss, part founder of the Police Orphanage. Public funeral Oct. 31.

— Oct. Electric light introduced in Royal Laboratory.

— Nov. Rev. J. Jordan appointed to Holy Trinity, Woolwich.

— Nov. 10. Judge Phillimore pronounced against both Princess Alice and Bywell Castle.

— Nov. 11 Plumstead Common transferred from Queen's College to Metropolitan Board.

— Nov. 14. Conclusion of Princess Alice inquest. Jury locked up from 5 p.m. to 7 a.m. 15 out of 19 jurors signed the verdict against the Princess Alice.

— Nov. 29. Death of Mr. Thos. Miles, of the Britannia Tavern, through a fall downstairs ; aged 65 years.

— Nov. 30. Mr. Gladstone's farewell to Greenwich. Meeting at Woolwich Skating Rink.

— Dec. 14. Death of H.R.H. the Princess Alice.

— Dec. 16. Opening of Wellington Soldiers' Institute.

1878—Dec. 23. Annie Lydia Laughton, aged 6, killed by her insane mother at 21, Armstrong Street. The mother was sent to an asylum.

— Dec. 23. Explosion of an " Afghan" rocket in the Royal Arsenal. Four men injured.

1879—Jan. 1. Presentation of £100 to Woolwich police, subscribed by the town.

— Jan. 2. Explosion of 38-ton gun on board H.M.S. Thunderer in Sea of Marmora.

— Jan. 9. Death of Mr. F. H. Banister, aged 60; funeral Jan. 14.

— Jan. 22. Disaster at Isandula. Busy preparations for Zulu campaign.

— Feb. 7. Death of Mr. A. H. Hiscock ; funeral Feb. 12.

— Feb. 9. Rev. J. Jordan commenced ministry at Holy Trinity.

— Mar. 14. Duke of Connaught married at Windsor.

— April. Military balloon committee instituted. " Talisman " balloon escaped April 25.

— April 1. Gen. J. Turner, C.B, succeeded Gen. Sir C. L D'Aguilar as commandant at Woolwich.

— April 9. Gunfire fixed at 1 p.m. and 9.30 p.m.

— April 13. Death of Dr. W. Stuart, aged 67 years. Funeral April 21.

— April 26. Arrival of four 100-ton guns at Royal Arsenal from Elswick. Purchased for £16,000 each from Vote of Credit.

— April 28. Fusee steamer attached to Arsenal.

— May. 1st Battn. Rifle Brigade and 1st Battn. 23rd Fusiliers together at Woolwich.

— May 2 (Sunday). Charlton pier destroyed by steamship Patrick Stewart.

— May 21. Prince Imperial killed in Zululand.

— June 6. Explosion at Home Office Magazine ; Mr. Dibblin

(foreman), Police Inspector Mc Elligot, and others injured

1879—June 24. 5th Lancers succeeded 18th Hussars at Woolwich.

— June 29. Death of Mr. G. Whale, sen., aged 79 ; funeral July 5.

— July 2. Memorial stone laid of Wesleyan Chapel, Plumstead Village.

— July 11. Body of the Prince Imperial landed at Royal Arsenal and conveyed to Chiselhurst ; funeral next day.

— July 31. Woolwich Coffee Tavern movement begun.

— Aug. 6. Lord Holmesdale and Kent Royal Arch Masons entertained at Plumstead Rink.

— Aug. 6. "Steeple Jack's" scaffold burnt at top of Cartridge Factory shaft.

— Aug. 14. Collision between Vesta and City of London in Barking Reach.

— Aug. 26. First wedding at St. James's, Plumstead.

— Sept. 11. Public opening of the High School for Boys, New Road.

— Oct. 8. Death of Mr. William Farnfield, aged 47. Public funeral at Charlton, Oct. 13.

— Oct. Lady Truro buried under the lawn at Falconhurst, Shooters' Hill.

— Oct. 15. Arrest of Henry Scott for burglaries at Plumstead.

— Oct. 23. Plumstead Road Board Schools opened.

— Oct. 27. Mr. G. Whale elected clerk of Plumstead Board.

— Oct. 28. Death of Mr. John Hammond, aged 63. Funeral, Nov. 3.

— Nov. 17. Roff's Pier, Woolwich, destroyed by steamship Canada.

— Nov. 25. Beresford Square market agitation. Interview of traders with Local Board.

— Nov. 29. High Street electric-lighted to counteract Beresford Square.

1879—Nov. Breech-loading guns ordered at the Arsenal.

— Dec. The "Winter of Fogs."

1880—Jan. 7. Blackheath High School for Girls opened by Princess Louise.

— Jan. 15. Reorganization of War Office clerks, Royal Arsenal.

— Jan. 17. Alexander Lindsay, aged 50, burnt at Raglan Road, Plumstead, in saving some children. Died Feb. 7th.

— Jan. 27. Fire at 28, High St.

— Jan. 27. Robert Sloper, 37, watchman at Roff's Pier, drowned during a fog.

— Jan. 29. Fire at Arnold's timber yard.

— Feb. 3. Second Thunderer gun burst to prove cause of previous accident by double loading.

— Feb. 5. Plumstead Relief Society formed.

— Feb. 15. Col. Stirling succeeded Col. King as Quartermaster Gen. at Woolwich.

— Feb. 19. Messrs. Wates and Watts, relieving officers, superannuated.

— Feb. 24. Military guard withdrawn from Arsenal.

— Mar. 1. Death of Major Ward Ashton, Riding Establishment, R.A., aged 43. Military funeral March 5th.

— Mar. 3. Death of Mr. George Barth, of Woolwich, in Bavaria, aged 46.

— Mar. 6. Italian 100-ton gun burst at Spezzia.

— Mar. 8. Five bodies of children found at shop of a North Woolwich undertaker, who absconded.

— Mar. 8. Two of the crew of the Lord Vivian drowned at the Arsenal.

— Mar. 19. Death of Mr. C. J. Carttar, coroner, aged 69 years.

— Mar. 21. Deptford Creek Bridge freed.

— Mar. 22. Hare Street Improvement "enquiry."

1880—Apr. 1. District Staff assumed duties of Coast Brigade, R.A., at Woolwich.

— Apr. 5. Mr. Gladstone, resigning Greenwich, elected for Midlothian.

— Apr. 8. Vestry decided to rebuild Woolwich church.

— Apr. 10. Action as to Plumstead sand-pits, "Jacobs v. Thrift and others" decided. Damages £250.

— Apr. 12. Explosion at Silvertown Creosote Works (Burt, Boulton, and Haywood's), eleven killed.

— April 17. Improvement of the Arsenal Station.

— April 19. Death of Mr. Wm. Watts, of the Admiral Hotel, Woolwich, aged 47 years.

— April 29. Poll for Coronership at Greenwich. Mr. E. A. Carttar, 728 ; Dr. Maxwell, 552 ; Mr. G. Collier, 123 ; Mr. H.W. Pook, 17.

— May 1. Gen. Sir John Adye, Governor, Royal Military Academy, appointed Surveyor General of Ordnance.

— May 1. Gen. Younghusband, R.A., superintendt. of Royal Gun Factories, retired ; succeeded by Col. Eardley Maitland, R.A.

— May 3. High School for Girls opened at Plumstead.

— May 3. Coffee Tavern movement started at Woolwich.

— May 6. Flooding the Albert Docks.

— May 8. "Princess Alice" memorial erected in Woolwich Cemetery by 23,000 subscriptions.

— May 18. Prince Ibrahim of Egypt passed from Royal Military Academy.

— May 20. Lieut. F. Pownall, R.A., of Woolwich, elected Grand Master of the Manchester Unity of Odd Fellows.

— May 25. Two men burnt to death at Silvertown.

1880—May 31. Death of Mr. A. Jessup, at Plumstead, aged 53. Buried at Ryarsh, June 5.

— June 1. Gen. Browne, R.E., appointed Govnr. of R.M. Academy.

— June 3. Sacrilege at St. Paul's, Charlton.

— June 3. Fire at Wilkie's, 44, Powis Street.

— June 15. Murder of Caroline Adams in Leather Bottle Tea Gardens, Erith, by Thos. Berry, a carpenter, who was executed July 27th, at Maidstone.

— June 24. Opening of Royal Albert Docks by the Duke and Duchess of Connaught.

— July. Reorganisation and consolidation of the Volunteers.

— July 11. Death of Canon Miller, at Greenwich, aged 66. Buried at Shooters' Hill Cemetery, July 16.

— July 12. Death of Mr. S. E. Hare, at Plumstead, aged 43. Buried July 17.

— July 14. Ordnance steamer Stanley commissioned at Arsenal.

— July 16. Death of Mr. Stephen Hudson, at Brighton, aged 45. Buried at Woolwich Cemetery, July 21.

— July 19. Coming of age of Mr. Maryon-Wilson. Fete at Old Charlton. Foundation stone of Assembly Room laid.

— July 20. Ordnance steamer Stanley's first voyage.

— July 22. Death of Mr. Joseph Cohen, at Woolwich, aged 80. Buried at Woolwich Cemetery, July 27.

— July 28. Attempt to enforce rights of way through Bostall Wood and High Grove Wood, Plumstead. Ended in apology.

— Aug. 16th Lancers stationed at Woolwich.

— Aug. 16. Reinforcements for India consequent on disaster at Maiwand. 23rd Fusiliers left Woolwich.

1880—Sept. 3. Breech-loading field guns (13-prs.) issued for service.
— Sept. 6. Death of Mr. R. Beaver, at Woolwich, aged 38. Buried at Woolwich Cemetery, Sept. 10.
— Sept. 8. Death of Mr. B. Wates.
— Sept. 13. 100-ton gun experiments at Royal Arsenal.
— Sept. 14. Lieut. Pownall, R.A. Grand Master of Odd Fellows, (M.U.) entertained at Skating Rink.
— Sept. 25. Woolwich steamboat Cupid run down by the D. W. Ward, screw steamer, off Woolwich.
— Oct. 2. Death of Mr. W. C. Taylor, at Woolwich, aged 61.
— Oct. 2. Death of Capt. Boylin, R.A., at Woolwich, aged 80.
— Oct. 6. Woolwich Chess Club established in William Street.
— Oct. 10. Orchard St. opened.
— Oct. 16. Death of Mr. G. J. Farnfield, at Woolwich, aged 42.
— Oct. 18. Public meeting to establish steam ferries at Woolwich. Attempt failed.
— Oct. 23. First funeral under the Burials Act at Plumstead.
— Oct. 30. Duke of Connaught laid memorial stone of Woolwich Coffee Tavern.
— Nov. The Rev. H. Hirsch, mission curate at Woolwich, appointed rector of St. Michael's, Cheapside.
— Dec. 1. Gen. Sir Frederick Roberts, R.A., entertained at Woolwich.
— Dec. 7. Explosion in Rocket Shed, Royal Arsenal. Three men (Knott, Wood, and Pomfret) injured.
— Dec. 10. Presentation to Mr. W. Price, principal foreman, Rl. Gun Factories, on retirement
— Dec. 13. First Hansom cab started at Woolwich.
— Dec. 20. Resignation of Mr. J. Smyth, Rl. Artillery bandmaster.

1880—Dec. 30. Thos. Hopperton found dead, shot through the head, in Wickham Lane, Plumstead. Open verdict.
— Dec. 31. Reinforcements left Woolwich for the Transvaal War.
1881—Jan. 4. Mr. J. R. Jolly resigned the chairmanship of the Greenwich Liberal Association.
— Jan. 6. Wedding of the Rev. J. Jordan and Miss Robertson at Woolwich Church
— Jan. 8. Fenian guard mounted over Plumstead magazines—first time since 1865.
— Jan. 18. Great snowstorm and floods. Tide rose 8 in. higher than on Nov. 15, 1875. Woolwich and Charlton Piers wrecked
— Jan. 21. Death, at Lewisham, of Mr. R. Ruegg, for 32 years editor of "*The Kentish Independent*," aged 65. Buried at St. Thomas's, Charlton.
— Feb. 8. Great fire at Victoria Dks.
— Feb. 18. J. Payne, (Forester), killed on the railway at Lewisham, aged 43.
— Feb. 18. 16th Lancers went from Woolwich to Ireland.
— Mar. 1. Woolwich and Plumstead tramway commenced.
— Mar. 11. Creation of Holy Trinity district, Woolwich.
— Mar. 18. Trees planted on Plumstead Common.
— Mar. 21. Rev. J. Jordan instituted vicar of the newly formed parish of Holy Trinity.
— Mar. 22. Death, at Lewisham, of Capt. Behenna, R.A., aged 62. Buried at Nunhead,
— Mar. 22. Deputation of sixty tradesmen to Woolwich Local Board as to steam ferry.
— Mar. 27. Rev. Chas. Box died, aged 86.
— Mar. 30. Public admitted to Plumstead Board.
— April 1. Gen. the Hon. E. T. Gage succeeded Gen. J. Turner in command of Woolwich District.

1881—April 2. Judgment delivered against the overseers of Woolwich in the Princess Alice case.

— April 3. Census Day.

— April 17. Salvation Army "attacked Woolwich."

— April 26. Opening of Charlton Village Hall.

— May 3. Mr. J. G. Burton, foreman, Royal Gun Factories, died, aged 43.

— May 6. Vicarage Road Board School opened.

— May 19. Presentation to Mr. J. Henry, principal foreman, Royal Laboratory, on retirement.

— May 28. First tram-car ran between Woolwich & Plumstead. Official inspection May 30, and public opening June 4.

— June 7. Death of Mr. B. Wells in New Zealand.

— June 14. Mr. J. R. Jolly elected member for Woolwich on Metropolitan Board, on retirement of Mr. W. P. Jackson.

— June 16. Sheriff's Court at Woolwich, to settle compensation for Hare Street improvement.

— June 22. Mr. E. L. Rumble elected surveyor of Plumstead, vice Mr. F. F. Thorne, retiring on a gratuity.

— June 26. Tram-car overturned in Plumstead Road. Several persons slightly hurt.

— June 28. First Wedding at Trinity Church, Woolwich.

— July 4. Death of Bandmaster Robshaw, 2nd K A.V.

— July 8. Three military prisoners escaped from R.A. guardroom, but were recaptured the same day.

— July 9. Local Volunteers attended the Windsor Review.

— July 12. Cromwell House for Working Boys at Woolwich op.

— July 21. Mr. C Jolly elected Vaccination Officer, Woolwich Union, vice C. Bishop, resigned.

1881—July 26. Murder of Fanny Mussel (or Vincent) in Cannon Row, Woolwich, by Geo. Durling, who was hanged on August 23.

— Aug. 9. Retirement of Mr. Geo. Hudson from public offices

— Aug. 19. Opening of Duke of Connaught Coffee Tavern, Woolwich.

— Sept. 6. King of the Sandwich Islands visited Woolwich.

— Sept. 14. Woolwich Liberal Association formed.

— Oct. Mr. S. Cook, the last parish constable of Plumstead, died.

— Oct. Lessness Heath Police Station established.

— Oct. 17. Foundation stone of Boys' High School, Brook Hill, laid by Lord Mayor McArthur.

— Oct. 18. Strike of servants at Woolwich Coffee Tavern.

— Oct. 28. Testimonial and dinner to Mr. F. Hart, station master.

— Nov. 1. Cavalier Zavertal appointed bandmaster Royal Artil.

— Nov. 3. Testimonial (£390) to Mr. Morris, manager, R.A. Mess.

— Nov. 12. Death of Mr. W. P. Jackson, aged 76. Public funeral at Woolwich Cemetery, November 19.

— Nov. 23. The Rev. W. N. Mc Guinness, vicar of All Saint's, Plumstead, died at sea.

— Nov. 24. Conduit Road Sunday School opened.

— Dec. 29. Mid-winter cricket match on Woolwich Common.

1882—Jan. 9. Dr. Potter's Anti-Catholic Lecture at the Coffee Tavern upset.

— Jan. 12. John Morby, one of the Plumstead Peculiar People, committed for trial for manslaughter of his child, aged 8. He was acquitted.

— Jan 18. Mr. J. R. Jolly, J.P., made steward of the Royal Manor of Greenwich.

— Jan. 28. Hare Street, Woolwich widened.

1882—Feb. 3. A French hermit discovered at Shooters' Hill.

— Feb. 9. Mr. Sampson elected Vestry Clerk of Woolwich, vice Peake, resigned.

— Feb. 14. Improvement of Woolwich Churchyard resolved upon.

— Feb. 15. Action "James v. Lloyd," breach of promise; damages £350.

— Feb. 23. A hunted deer captured in the Arsenal.

— Feb. 26. Death at Bexley Heath of Mr. John Barnett, late Woolwich surveyor, aged 76. Buried at Wool. Cemetery Mar. 3.

— Feb. 27. Suicide of Mr. Compton at Charlton, aged 62.

— Mar. 4. Opening of Boys' High School, Brook Hill, by Lord Mayor Ellis.

— Mar. 8. Coldstream Guards march to Woolwich for Ireland, lunched at R.A. Barracks.

— Mar. 12. First joint church parade of troops and volunteers (2nd K.A.V.) at Woolwich.

— Mar. 18. Reorganization of Artillery. Depot of R.H.A., &c., established at Woolwich.

— Mar. 25. Plumstead Common bankrupts released from bills of sale.

— Mar. 28. Wiltshire Regiment (62nd) arrived at Woolwich.

— Apr. 12. First lady (Miss Evins) elected on Woolwich Guardians.

— Apr. 13. Greenwich and Woolwich tramway begun.

— Apr. 13. Mr. Thos. Smith died at Shakespeare Tavern, Woolwich, aged 42.

— Apr. 26. Last "visitation" day at Greenwich.

— Apr. 27. Marriage of the Rev. Dr. Rentoul.

— May 20. Death of Mr. A. Moody, registrar, aged 74.

— June. Parliamentary commission appointed as to state of the Thames.

1882—June 1. Mr. T.W. Anderson elected registrar, Woolwich Dockyard district, vice Moody.

— June 6. Plumstead ceased to take road material from Plumstead Common.

— June 6. Deputation to Board of Trade as to workmen's trains.

— June 12. Mr. W. Mills died of hydrophobia at Plumstead.

— June 13. Death of Mr. Francis J. Sales, aged 32, at Margate. Buried at Charlton, June 19.

— June 19. Improvement of Church Street, Woolwich.

— June 17. Death of Mr. W. S. Robinson, aged 81. Buried at Woolwich Cemetery, June 22.

— June 20. Preparations commenced for Campaign in Egypt.

— July. H.M. Treasury voted £100 towards " Princess Alice " expenses.

— July 4. Clacton Railway opd.

— July 22. Conservative demonstration at Charlton Park. Sir Stafford Northcote the Earl of Stanhope, and eight other M.P's. present.

— July 30. Embarkation of Duke of Connaught at North Woolwich for Egypt. Prince and Princess of Wales, Prince Albert Victor, Prince George, Duke of Edinburgh, Duchess of Connaught, and Duke of Cambridge were present.

— Aug. 1. Great activity at Woolwich, owing to war in Egypt.

— Aug. 5. Woolwich buys a steam roller.

— Aug. 23. Cetewayo at Woolwich Arsenal.

— Aug. 24. Opening of the New Bull Inn, Shooters' Hill.

— Sept. 4. Plague of flies at Woolwich.

— Sept. 11. Opening of Hundred of Hoo Railway.

— Sept. 13. Battle of Tel-el-Kebir.

— Oct. North Kent Coursing Club, first meet.

1882—Oct. 10. Louisa Jane Taylor charged with poisoning Mary Ann Tregillis with sugar of lead, at Plumstead. Mrs. Tregillis died Oct. 23, and Taylor was hanged at Maidstone, Jan. 2, 1883.

— Oct. 10. Woolwich voted an address to Sir John Adye on his return from Egypt. Presented at the Town Hall, Oct. 27.

— Oct. 14. Fred Leslie, the Woolwich actor, appeared as " Rip Van Winkle," at Comedy Theatre, London.

— Oct. 24. First troops returned to Woolwich from Egypt.

— Nov. 4. Murder of Corp. Edgar (62nd, Wiltshire Reg.) in Cambridge Barracks, Woolwich, by Corp. Alfred Harris, of same regiment. He was convicted, but death sentence commuted to life imprisonment.

— Nov. 18. Special holiday at Arsenal in recognition of services during war. The Queen's review in London.

— Nov. 18. Proposed new railway and subway under Thames at Woolwich.

— Nov. 21. Tramway from Greenwich to Woolwich and Plumstead opened.

— Nov. 23. Indian Contingent visited Royal Arsenal.

— Nov. 26. Mr. E. Hughes elected on London School Board for Greenwich.

— Nov. Piece of Royal Arsenal granted to Plumstead for stoneyard.

— Dec. 13. Death of Mr. W. T. Henley, aged 73.

— Dec. 17. Burning of Cotopaxi in Albert Docks.

— Dec. 26. Death of Mr. Henry Hanks, of Carmel Chapel, aged 71 years.

— Dec. 30. Woolwich " Parliament " established.

1883. — Jan. 4. Death of Mr. Henry Shersby, aged 60. Buried in Woolwich Churchyard Jan. 9. Estate £130,000.

1883—Jan. 12. Col. Duncan sent to Egypt to organize Artillery.

— Jan. 12. Prince of Wales unveiled monument of Prince Imperial at Royal Military Academy.

— Jan. 16. Proposed railway and subway under the Thames at Woolwich abandoned.

— Jan. 27. Death of Mr. F. C. Buchanan, aged 63.

— Jan. 29. Death of Mr. Wm. Price (late R.G.F.) at Sunderland, aged 56.

— Feb. 7. Thursday closing at 5 p.m. instituted at Woolwich.

— Feb. 9. Death of Mr. G. H. Fisk, Workhouse master, aged 45. Succeeded by Mr. J. E. Rigden March 8.

— Feb. 11. Testimonial to Detective Sergt. Davis.

— Mar. 17. Foundation laid of St. John's Church, Plumstead.

— Mar. 31. Funeral of Major McGrath : died 22nd.

— Mar. 31. Death of the Rev. T. Tuffield, Registrar, aged 59. Buried at Woolwich Cemetery April 7.

— April 1. General H. A. Smith made commandant of Woolwich, vice the Hon. E. T. Gage, promoted

— April 2. Opening of Wood Street Schools.

— April 5. Captured dynamite brought to Royal Arsenal. Destroyed.

— April 12. Mrs. Tuffield elected registrar for East Woolwich.

— April 20. Meeting to found Plumstead Almshouses.

— April 24. Wedding of the Rev. J. O. Bent and Miss Harrison at Charlton.

— April 26. Gas exhibition at Woolwich.

— April 27. New opera by Cav. Zavertal at Garrison Theatre.

1883— April 27. Fall of a house in St. Mary Street

— May 12. Death of Mr. J. J. Banister, aged 51.

— May 13. Death of Mr. Z. Parkes, aged 79.

— June 2. Hon. Canon Anson, Rector of Woolwich, resigned to take mission work in Canada. Farewell service July 29. Succeeded by the Rev. S. Gilbert Scott, of Battersea.

— July 4. Retirement of Mr. J. Boustred, chief clerk at police court.

— July 13. Death of Mr. W. Akers, aged 75.

— July 18. Woolwich breach of promise case, " West v. Sales," damages £70.

— July 19. Mr. A. Burnett elected Vestry Clerk of Charlton in succession to his father. Burnett, 12 ; Muskett, 6 ; Hughes, 6.

— July 22. Death of Mr. H. Mabbett, aged 53. Military and masonic funeral, July 28.

— July 25. Suicide of Dr. Purland, aged 82.

— July 29. Farewell sermons of Canon Anson and Rev. R. T. Love, curate.

— Aug. 1. " Old gunners' dinner" established.

— Aug. 1. Institution of parcels post.

— Aug. 1. Induction of Rev. S. G. Scott, of Battersea, rector of Woolwich.

1883— Aug. 3. Canon Anson left Woolwich for Canada. Rev. R. T. Love, curate, became rector of Cowlinge.

— Aug. 8. Death of Mr. J. Furlong, aged 72. Funeral Aug. 13.

— Aug. 13. Fire in Bostall Wood.

— Aug. 18. Fire in Model-room, R M. Academy.

1883—Aug. 22. Suicide of Louisa Walder, barmaid, Old Charlton.

— Aug. 29. Mr. J. R. Jolly, J.P., elected Chairman of Woolwich Local Board.

— Sept. 9. First sermon at Woolwich of Rev. S. G. Scott, rector.

— Sept. 21. Death of Mr. Chas. Sargent, jun., aged 32.

— Sept. 24. Restoration of Trinity Church ordered.

— Sept. 24. Explosion of the Rl. Arsenal Rocket Store. Richard Stevenson and Edward Carlick, killed. For nearly an hour, war rockets, to the number of 500, were discharged in all directions for miles round, creating great peril and alarm and doing some damage to property, but no further personal injury.

— Sept. 27. Death of Mr. Samuel Hellard, aged 82.

— Oct. 2. Death of Mr. J. K. Paine, aged 53. Public funeral.

— Oct. 17. Death of Mr. James Wates, of Sydenham, aged 52.

— Nov. 2. Metropolitan Board decided to establish Woolwich Steam Ferry.

— Nov. 5. Restoration of Woolwich Church ordered.

— Nov. 19. Death of Mr George Hudson, aged 77 years. Funeral November 22.

— Nov. 19. Death of Sir William Siemans

— Nov. 21. Bazaar at St. Andrew's Church, opened by Lord Mayor Fowler.

— Nov. 27. London Steamboat Company failed.

— Dec. 4. Death of Mr. J. C. Jack, sec. Arsenal Foremen's Association Funeral Dec 8.

— Dec. 12. Death of Mr. E. B. Sargent, Clerk to Guardians, aged 57.

Elections for the Borough of Greenwich since the Reform Act of 1832.

1832 (Dec.)			1857 (Mar.)		
*J. W. D. Dundas	(L)	1633	*Sir W. Codrington	(L)	2985
*E. G. Barnard	(L)	1442	*John Townsend	(L)	2784
John Angerstein	(L)	1033	M. Chambers	(L)	2065
F. G. Hammond	(L)	15	1859 (April).		
1835 (Jan.)			*D. Salomons	(L)	3873
*J. Angerstein	(L)	1826	*W. Angerstein	(L)	3520
*E. G. Barnard	(L)	1102	M. Chambers	(L)	1718
M. W. Attwood	(C)	1063	Sir J. H. Maxwell	(C)	1031
1837 (Aug.)			1865 (July).		
*M. W. Attwood	(C)	1368	*D. Salomons	(L)	4499
*E. G. Barnard	(L)	1194	*Sir C. Bright	(L)	3691
Capt. C. Napier	(L)	1158	Sir J. H. Maxwell	(C)	2328
1841 (July).			J. B. Langley	(L)	190
*Capt. W. D. Dundas	(L)	1747	Capt. D. Harris	(L)	1
*E. G. Barnard	(L)	1592	1868 (Nov.)		
Sir G. Cockburn	(C)	1274	*Sir D. Salomons	(L)	6685
1847 (Aug.)			*W. E. Gladstone	(L)	6386
*Admiral Dundas	(L)	2409	Sir H. W. Parker	(C)	4704
*E. G. Barnard	(L)	1511	Viscount Mahon	(C)	4372
D. Salomons	(L)	1236	On death of Sir D. Salomons :		
On the decease of Mr. Barnard,			1873 (Aug.)		
1551 (June)			*T. W. Boord	(C)	4525
*D. Salomons	(L)	2165	J. B. Langley	(L)	2379
D. W. Wire	(L)	1278	W. Angerstein	(L)	1063
On Admiral Dundas resigning,			Sir J. Bennett	(L)	324
1852 (Feb.)			R. Coningsby	(LC)	30
*Admiral H. Stewart	(L)	2956	H. Pook	(C)	27
Montague Chambers	(L)	1211	1874 (Feb.)		
1852 (July).			*T. W. Boord	(C)	6193
*Peter Rolt	(C)	2415	*W. E. Gladstone	(L)	5968
*M. Chambers	(L)	2360	J. E. Liardet	(C)	5561
Admiral Stewart	(L)	2026	J. B. Langley	(L)	5255
D. Salomons	(L)	1102	1880 (April).		
On Mr. Rolt accepting a Government contract :			*T. W. Boord	(C)	9243
			*Baron H. de Worms	(C)	9240
1857 (Feb.)			J. E. Saunders	(L)	8152
*Sir W. Codrington	(L)	w.o.	W. H. Stone	(L)	8141

An asterisk (*) signifies elected.

POPULATION, &c.

	Census 1841.	Census 1851.	Census 1861.	Census 1871.	Census 1881.
Charlton............	2655	4818	8472	9503	10930
Kidbrook	597	460	804		
Woolwich Dockyard..	25785	32367	22919	17229	17650
Woolwich Arsenal ...			18776	18319	18950
Plumstead West	2816	8373	11332	13028	14009
Plumstead East			13170	15290	19243
Totals	31853	46018	75473	73369	80782

School Board Elections.—Greenwich Division, (4 *Members.)*

1870.		1876—*continued.*	
Miss Davies	10,061	Mr. G. B. Richardson	14,357
Mr. Macgregor	7,828	Rev. C. F. S. Money	14,215
Canon Miller	7,296	Rev. Dr. Wallace	7,211
Rev. B. Waugh	7,143	1879.	
Mr. Glennie	6,250	Mr. H. Gover	
Seven other candidates.		Mr. J. E. Saunders	No
1873.		Mr. G. B. Richardson	contest
Rev. A. Legge	19,764	Rev. T. D. C. Morse	
Mr. Gover	13,909	1882.	
Rev. B. Waugh	9,971	Mr. E. Hughes	22,162
Mr. Broadhurst	5,535	Mr. J. E. Saunders	9,496
Miss Guest	3,864	Mr. H. Gover	9,244
1876.		Rev. T. D. C. Morse	5,890
Mr. H. Gover	15,479	Mr. G. B. Richardson	4,990
Mr. J. E. Saunders	15,305		

TABLE OF DISTANCES FROM WOOLWICH.

The following table has been compiled by an able surveyor from careful measurements on the Ordnance map. The distances given must be regarded as approximate only, a few yards more or less, but, with this reservation, they may be pronounced correct. The measurements are taken in all cases from the Main Gate of the Royal Arsenal, in Beresford Square.

PLACE.	No. of miles from Arsenal Gate.
Belvedere (Belvedere House)	4
Bexley (Old Bexley Village)	6
Bexley Heath (the Lord Hill)	5
Blackheath (St. Germain's Terrace)	3
Blackheath Village	3½
Bromley (Market Place)	7½
Charlton (Old Church)	1¾
Chislehurst (the Church)	6½
Crayford	6
Croydon (Town)	12
Deptford (Broadway)	4½
Dartford (The Bull)	8
Eltham (Church)	3
Erith	5½
Footscray (Village)	7
Forest Hill (Station)	7
Gravesend	13
Greenwich (Railway Station)	4
London (Royal Exchange)	9
Lee Green	4
Lewisham (the Station)	4
New Cross (New Cross Gate)	5½
Northfleet	12
Sidcup (the Black Horse)	6¼
Sydenham	7¾
Welling (the Village)	3¼

A WOOLWICH ACTOR.

MR. FRED LESLIE, whose portrait we are enabled to publish by the courtesy of the *Sporting and Dramatic News* and by the skill of its artist, was introduced both to the world and to the stage at Woolwich. Like Mr. Sothern, of "Dundreary" fame—and many other great men, who have either avowed or concealed the fact—he was born on that day of the year which according to the official returns produces the lowest birthrate, namely, "All Fools Day," for it was on April

FRED LESLIE.

1st, 1856, that he first saw the light. From his earliest boyhood his taste and talent for dramatic representation were mani-
fested, not unfrequently to the anxiety of his friends, and his
powers of mimicry and wit were, even in youth, quite remarkable. His early genius was conspicuous at many modest
concerts and readings in which he took part, and he made his
first public attempt as an actor when quite a lad at the Lecture
Hall, Nelson Street, Woolwich, playing the part of "Distafina,"
in *Bombastes Furioso*. Prior to this, however, his prevailing
inclination asserted itself while at school in France, where he
acted the French *role* of "Pierre," in *Les deux Pigeons*. His
apprenticeship to the art and calling of the drama may, however, be said to have been served at the handsome and convenient Garrison Theatre in the Royal Artillery Barracks, at
Woolwich, where he was for two years a member of a stock company of amateurs. In this connection he cleverly enacted a
lengthy repertoire of "first old men," his strong talent for
character-acting giving him naturally this curious but fortunate
bent. His chief success at this time was "Sir Peter Teazle,"
in the *School for Scandal* (played when he was under twenty-
one years of age) a success which has since been amply verified
in London by the public and the press. Designed by parental
dispositions for the auctioneer's rostrum as the fitting theatre for
his public displays, he was allowed to waste eight months assisting
at the knocking down of lots, but, to the trouble of his family,
he threw up his hopes of advancement in that direction, and,
soon afterwards, hating idleness, he found some scope for his
restless spirit in the firm of Hobson & Son, his brothers, well-
known and extensive army contractors in London and Woolwich.
The inference to be derived as to family name is perfectly justified. "Leslie" is the name which he assumed from mere fancy
when he played as an amateur, and it has borne him well through
the world to fame and honour. In the midst of ledgers and in-
voices he fancied for a time that he had found a vocation, but
his heart panted still for the footlights; and, at length, being
convinced that it was useless to struggle against his fate, he took
competent advice, and, after several disheartening refusals (since
bitterly repented by their authors), he obtained his first London
engagement at the Royalty Theatre, in February, 1878, to play
"Colonel Hardy" to Mr. Lionel Brough's "Paul Pry," at the
noble salary of £1 a week! From that day his fortune was
made, every step having been upwards on the ladder of renown,

until he has reached almost, if not quite, the topmost round. His visits to America, though short, were rich in opportunities, and his reception by the hospitable Yankees was almost enough to tempt him to remain, for they declared that "Leslie was Wallack in his young days," and that England had sent them nothing so good for many years. But Leslie had attractions strong to draw him home again across the Atlantic, and success after success has left him no chance of regretting his return. Many triumphs scored at various London theatres have rendered him one of the most popular of London actors, and he is almost equally favoured in such of the principal provincial centres which he has had occasion to visit. In the profession he is also held in high esteem, his geniality and want of assumption being as strongly marked as his rare ability. The versatility of his genius has never been better displayed than in the part of "Rip Van Winkle" in the comic opera of that name at the Comedy Theatre, and it has been asserted that no other living actor could have so well essayed the mingled drollery and pathos, the transition from youth to age, the music of the earlier scenes and the cracked notes of the concluding ones—all requiring a combination of skill seldom to be found in one person. His voice is a baritone of unusual compass and purity. Neither are his talents confined to the stage. He is an artist in oils, and his rooms are decorated with many canvasses of his own brushing, including portraits of his friends Henry Irving and Harry Paulton. He also writes songs and composes the music; and one humorous ditty, his "Love in the Lowther," has run through several editions.

Lightning Source UK Ltd.
Milton Keynes UK
UKOW07f1834170216

268604UK00006B/96/P